FROM OEDIPUS TO MOSES

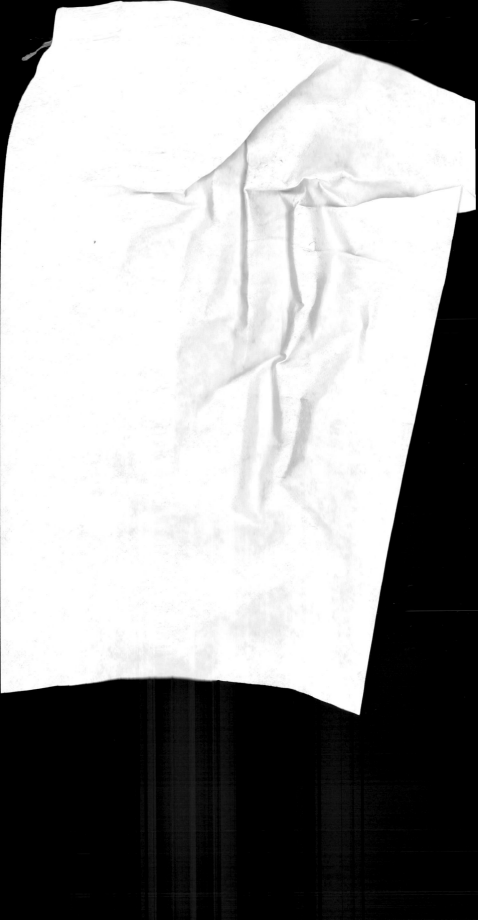

FROM OEDIPUS TO MOSES

Freud's Jewish Identity

BY MARTHE ROBERT

Translated by Ralph Manheim

Originally published as
d'Oedipe à Moïse: Freud et la conscience juive

ANCHOR BOOKS
Anchor Press/Doubleday
Garden City, New York
1976

d'Oedipe à Moïse: Freud et la conscience juive was originally published by Calmann-Lévy, Paris, France. Copyright © Calmann-Lévy, 1974

Anchor Books Edition
1976

I wish to thank Wolfgang Sauerlander for assembling the English equivalents of the Freud quotations in this book and Harry Franz Lobner, Curator of the Freud House, Vienna, for putting the facilities under his care at our disposal.

R.H.

LIBRARY OF CONGRESS CATALOGING IN PUBLICATION DATA

ROBERT, MARTHE.
FROM OEDIPUS TO MOSES.

TRANSLATION OF D'OEDIPE À MOÏSE.
INCLUDES BIBLIOGRAPHICAL REFERENCES.
I. FREUD, SIGMUND, 1856–1939. 2. PSYCHOANALYSIS.
3. JEWS—PSYCHOLOGY. I. TITLE.
BF173.F85R6213   150'.19'52
ISBN 0-385-00064-2
LIBRARY OF CONGRESS CATALOG CARD NUMBER 76–3125

for Michel

CONTENTS

I

OEDIPUS-FREUD, SON OF JAKOB

The intimate relationship between psychoanalysis and the "Jewish spirit" is so obvious that few of those who refer to it stop to define the "Jewish spirit" or to ask how it has been transmitted from generation to generation.[1] And it goes without saying that different writers mention this relationship for different reasons and accordingly draw different conclusions from it. Some take it in a frankly pejorative sense and after disparaging psychoanalysis as a science proceed to denigrate it as a "Jewish science"; others, on the contrary, take it as one of many proofs that the "Jewish spirit" has served at all times to shake the world out of its slumber and to revolutionize human thought, and group Freud with Bergson and Einstein among the Jewish thinkers who by their extraordinary boldness have played so great a part in the growth of the new era. Though radically opposed, these two attitudes are identical in one point: they fail to define the "Jewish spirit" and leave it in a zone of shadow far more conducive to emotional outbursts than to the critical examination of ideas.

Though he does not dwell on the subject, Freud often speaks of it, especially in his letters and in his *Autobiographical Study*. Indeed, he was the first to relate his discoveries to intellectual and moral traits which, he believed, derive from his origins. Not that he had any exact idea as to how the "Jewish spirit" inspired his theories or seriously appraised his indebtedness to any specific aspect of the Jewish tradition. But he was convinced that the fact of being a Jew was an enormous help to him in his fight against widely held prejudices; and that if he was able in the end to gain acceptance for his "bit of truth," it was largely because he had

3

inherited the courage of rebellion. In short, he adapted to his own personal situation the theory[2] that the Jewish mind is essentially nonconformist, hence prophetic in the sense that its freedom from the intellectual tyrannies of the dominant society has always enabled it to innovate by working with the most fruitful ideas available. Thus in his address to the B'nai B'rith—a Jewish liberal organization in which he was active for twenty years and to which he belonged up to the time of his death—he attributes the two qualities that he regards as decisive for the development of his work essentially to his "Jewish nature." "Because I was a Jew I found myself free from many prejudices which restricted others in the use of their intellect; and as a Jew I was prepared to join the Opposition and to do without agreement with the 'compact majority.' "[3] Here, as in the passage in *My Life and Psychoanalysis*[4] dealing with the racial prejudice which to his surprise and dismay he encountered the moment he entered the university, he considers Judaism chiefly in contrast to gentile society and not essentially from the standpoint of its own historic value or spiritual message. When it comes to sound thinking, the Jew has two advantages over others: his vision is not clouded by the scraps of beliefs, the vestiges of dogmas and superstitions, that clutter up the mind of the most advanced Christian, even when he supposes that he has been freed from tenacious prejudices bound up with his civilization; moreover, the Jew is not tempted to imitate the conformism of those around him, or if he is so tempted, the hostility and contempt of his adoptive environment soon send him back to his original self. Over against the obscure intellectual constraints in which the "others" remain imprisoned, the Jew is free in two respects, first in regard to his own spiritual heritage, which does not necessarily distort his judgment, and second in regard to the Christian heritage, to which in any event he has no recognized claim. It is primarily, perhaps solely, thanks to this twofold freedom that psychoanalysis was able to impose itself as a science and develop its arms for the attack that still remains to be made on the last frontiers of the mind.

Not only does Freud speak of a "Jewish nature," specially equipped to take its place in the forefront of intellectual struggle; he also draws the radical conclusion that psychoanalysis could be invented only by a Jew and that this explains why despite its urgency this investigation of the human psyche was so long delayed. Why, he asked Pastor Pfister in the course of a friendly argument, didn't one of those pious men create psychoanalysis? Why did it have to wait for an absolutely irreligious Jew?[5]

Just as psychoanalysis needed a Jew to call it to life, so Jews, despite the internal resistance which they like all other people encounter in the difficult work of analysis, find their way instinctively to the theory, whereas a non-Jew, if he is truly to follow Freud and accept his manner of thinking, must in addition surmount all manner of obstacles arising from the burden of prejudices and mystical chimeras that he has been unable to cast off. However sincere Jung, for example, may have been—and at first Freud had no doubt of his sincerity—he could not take the decisive leap unaided, because, faced with the most shocking revelations of the "Jewish science," he remained in large part captive to his own archaeology. Hence Freud's advice to Karl Abraham in 1908 when Abraham, who distrusted the new recruit's theoretical deviations—and not without reason—expressed his unwillingness to do anything to forestall a conflict: "Please be tolerant," Freud wrote, "and do not forget that it is really easier for you than it is for Jung to follow my ideas, for in the first place you are completely independent, and in the second place you are closer to my intellectual constitution because of racial kinship, while he as a Christian and a pastor's son finds his way to me only against great inner resistances. His association with us is the more valuable for that. I nearly said that it was only by his appearance on the scene that psycho-analysis escaped the danger of becoming a Jewish national affair."[6] In another letter he is even more explicit.

"On the whole it is easier for us Jews, as we lack the mystical element."[7] Thus the formative years of the psycho-analytical movement are characterized by a striking contrast: while an Abraham was able to follow Freud without difficulty, or at least without feeling too disoriented, it cost Jung an enormous effort to eliminate the vestiges of religion and the largely unconscious archaic images that influenced his scientific attitudes and led to continual deviations from Freud. Of this Abraham was well aware; he knew that his closeness to Freud was due in part to their common origins. "After all," he wrote, "our Talmudic mode of thought cannot disappear just like that."[8] With this mention of the Talmud the argument ended for the time being, but Jung soon succumbed to the "mystical element" and Freud was sadly confirmed in his belief that the "others" would find it hard to adjust to psychoanalysis.[9]

In speaking of the Jewish origins of psychoanalysis, Freud's main purpose was to suggest that the Jews and the new science were in a similar situation in the face of a hostile, contemptuous, or at best indifferent world, which accepts innovations only if it can square them with its own prejudices. He does not discuss the substance of the kinship between Jewishness and psychoanalysis, but, at least to judge by the letters at our disposal, speaks only of the strong, almost involuntary ties created by anti-Semitism.[10] Immediately after the appearance of *The Interpretation of Dreams*, certain of Freud's students who were versed in Hebrew began searching the ancient writings for parallels. For, amid the vast body of rabbinical literature, it is indeed possible to find precepts and maxims that come curiously close to Freud's most daring ideas. The rabbis attached great importance to the interpretation of dreams, to sexuality and married life, and in general to down-to-earth day-to-day existence. Furthermore, parallels can be drawn between Freudian symbolism and the theories of words and numbers, which were the principal instrument of rabbinical exegesis.[11] All this, to be sure, makes it possible to draw ingenious correspondences, but amounts to little more than doubtful speculation, first of all because those who make much of analogies based on approximate resemblances say nothing of the enormous gulf between Freud's purposes and those of the rabbis, and also because in all likelihood very similar and equally inconclusive parallels might be found in very different traditions. In any event, Freud, though amused by such studies, took no active part in them, and it seems hardly surprising that an "absolutely irreligious Jew" (as he was and wanted to be) felt no need to stress the local color of his scientific discoveries. To his mind they had value only in so far as they contributed to the broadening of scientific knowledge and could thus lay claim to a universality transcending the private circumstances of their author.

We shall see that, apart from its intellectual and moral motivations, Freud's coolness to the specific content of Judaism had more secret roots. Because of it, Freud never really tried to define his exact place in contemporary Jewry; nor did he ever explain how it came about that psychoanalysis, though profoundly marked by its Jewish origins, has something essential to say about mankind in general, quite apart from all ethnic, historic, cultural, and social variables. These two questions—which are among others the subject of the present book—deserve to be taken seriously, not only because they relate to the situation of modern Jewish thought, but also because they point to a specifically modern paradox, the paradox of a localized particular giving rise to something universal.

That the situation of psychoanalysis in contemporary Jewry could nevertheless be seen from within and not only in its relations with the majority bloc of "the others" was dimly recognized by Franz Kafka, a writer utterly disinclined to play an active role in "Jewish national affairs" or to delve deeply into Freud, but who, thanks to the lucidity he derived from his deliberate aloofness, is a most revealing witness in these matters as in many others. Kafka held that psychoanalysis was not primarily a general theory of the human psyche; that a Jew in any event must not regard it as such, for in so doing he would be turning his

7

back on reality by making one of those premature leaps that arrest thought and thereby lead to the worst of intellectual sins (Kafka's hero is always an individual who generalizes instead of living: that is his "offense," which life automatically punishes). According to Kafka, Freud's work was, rather, a chapter of Jewish history written for the present generation, in a sense the latest of Talmudic treatises, and though Freudian psychology might have other implications, this was at least its profoundest justification. In a letter of December 1922 to Franz Werfel, Kafka spoke of his aversion for *Schweiger*, a play in which Werfel, according to Kafka, falsified and degraded the sufferings of their generation: "It is no pleasure to busy oneself with psychoanalysis, and I keep as far away from it as possible, but it has at least as much reality as this generation. The Jews have always produced their joys and their sorrows at almost the same time as the Rashi commentary relating to them, and here again they have done so.[12] We see that Kafka follows neither Freud, who mentions only the contingent, though specific, aspects of the Jewish character of psychoanalysis, nor those who think they find proof of it in the rabbinical literature.[13] In Kafka's view, the Freudian doctrine finds its meaning primarily in the context of present-day Jewish life, which like all life is made up of joys and sorrows, but with the difference that, obliged since time immemorial to provide its own commentary, it has always been a written life, produced not before but *almost at the same time* as the writings that explain it. Kafka does not name these sorrows and joys, of which Freud is today the interpreter (and in a sense the prophet, because they occurred some time after his explanation), but it is clear from an earlier letter relating to the heart of the problem that he knew whereof he spoke, at least with regard to the "sorrows," for, as we know, "joys" were not exactly his forte. A year before, Kafka wrote to Max Brod on the subject of a book by Karl Kraus,[14] which, Kafka believed, revealed the ingrained defects of German-Jewish literature, and on a deeper level the crisis of the assimilated Jews, corroded from within by insoluble problems of language: "What appeals to me more than psychoanalysis [in this book] is the observation that the father complex from which more than one Jew draws his spiritual nourishment relates not to the innocent father but to the father's Judaism. What most of those who began to write in German wanted was to break with Judaism, generally with the vague approval of their fathers (this vagueness is the revolting part of it). That is what they wanted, but their hind legs were bogged down in their fathers' Judaism, and their front legs could find no new ground. The resulting despair was their inspiration."[15] In this strangely intransigent passage—addressed, it should not be forgotten, to Max Brod, a writer who, especially because of the blissful naïveté of his style, must himself be classified among the torn souls described above—Kafka is not so much concerned with judging individual works of German-Jewish literature as with characterizing a basic dilemma which most German-Jewish writers misrepresented or shrugged off when they did not pass it over in silence. By this failure to deal with their own situation, Kafka held, they condemned their work to insignificance. It was not a matter of talent or hard work; the evil was fundamental and would still have been incurable even if the works in question had been works of genius.

This literary failing had its source in the life of the German-Jewish community. The whole younger generation might have showered their elders with the reproaches that Kafka addressed to Hermann, his father, in the famous *Letter* he wrote at the age of thirty-six in an attempt to unravel the causes of their estrangement.[16] Typical of an irresolute generation that let itself be tossed back and forth between contrary choices, Hermann Kafka was by no means the innocent father whom the Greek Oedipus was destined to kill. On the contrary, he was doubly guilty, guilty of being what he was and guilty of not being really or sufficiently what he was; of remaining too much of a Jew to break with a bloodless tradition, in which his children saw nothing but an empty aping of ritual; but not enough of a Jew to hand down a possibility of authentic self-contained and self-justifying existence. "I found as little escape from you in Judaism," wrote Kafka in accusation. "Here some measure of escape would have been thinkable in principle, moreover, it would have been thinkable that we might both have found each other in Judaism or that we even might have begun from there in harmony. But what sort of Judaism was it that I got from you?" Undoubtedly the father himself had little to give, and that little was not transmissible: "You really had brought some traces of Judaism with you from the ghetto-like community; it was not much and it dwindled a little more in the city and during your military service; but still, the impressions and memories of your youth did just about suffice for some sort of Jewish life. . . ." If Kafka's father had valued the scraps of tradition that were still alive in him he might have taught his son to love them, but since they left him cold, they never meant anything more to his children than incomprehensible obligations and empty gestures which they could only regard as revolting hypocrisy: "It was also impossible to make a child, overacutely observant from sheer nervousness, understand that the few flimsy gestures you performed in the name of Judaism, and with an indifference in keeping with their flimsiness, could have any higher meaning. For you they had meaning as little souvenirs of earlier times, and that was why you wanted to pass them on to me, but since they no longer had any intrinsic value, even for you, you could do this only through persuasion or threat: on the one hand, this could not be successful, and on the other, it had to make you angry with me on account of my apparent obstinacy. . . ." But Kafka makes it clear that all this was not an isolated case. ". . . It was much the same with a large section of this transitional generation of Jews, which had migrated from the still comparatively devout countryside to the cities," so that, especially in German countries, the Jewish family lived in a chronic state of crisis. By the fault of all the Hermann Kafkas who have brought a little authentic Judaism from their "rural ghettos," yet demand of their children a *vague* fidelity to tradition while at the same time consenting *vaguely* to the children's desire to break with that same tradition ("this vagueness is the revolting part of it"), the sons, whatever they may do, are unhappy animals, doomed to live between two worlds and to be taken in by their own duplicity. Hence the son's revolt against the man who, though himself a victim of circumstances, sinning only by lukewarmness or vulgar opportunism, nevertheless bears the main responsibility for a sterile conflict, productive only of imposture and despair. The father, to be sure, can also be the source of a dubious sort of inspiration, but this was far from attenuating his responsibility in Kafka's eyes. Psychoanalysis deals precisely with this father and its first task, quite apart from its more general message, was to explain this very definite conflict to a whole generation of spiritually and socially uprooted Jews.[17]

It will no doubt be argued that Kafka's passionate indictment of his father smacks of typical neurotic hypocrisy, since from the "Oedipus complex" he removes the incest motif without which it would not be a "complex" and speaks as an accuser, although in fact it is he and he alone who feels accused (and we know how epically he reverses the situation in his books). Above all, it will be said that since in Freud's mind psychoanalysis was from the start something very different from a dramatic controversy between a Jewish father and a Jewish son, capable neither of total reconciliation nor total rupture, to reduce psychoanalysis to so narrowly localized a context is tantamount to thinking it out of existence. Both these objections are justified. Nevertheless, Kafka's neurosis provided an extraordinary precision instrument with which to discern the hidden reality beneath conventional images and ideas; and though it is true that psychoanalysis as a science must and does confine itself to the universal, the fact remains that it essentially owes its existence to its creator's self-analysis, and that the central figure in this unprecedented experience was not an indeterminate father, but necessarily Jakob Freud, a Jewish father, a "vague" father who, from what we know of his times and birthplace, must also have left his son in a state of suspension between two histories, two cultures, two irreconcilable forms of thought. True, the "Oedipus complex," which today is generally acknowledged to be the human drama par excellence, draws its name from a cultural sphere which Jakob Freud did not even dream of entering, but this borrowed name must not blind us to the nature of the primary experience that gave rise to the concept.[18] To Sigmund Freud, the primordial murdered father was Jakob Freud, the Galician Jew, and not a legendary Greek king. In this light, Kafka's provocative sentence about the "Rashi commentary" takes on an infinitely profounder significance than many an abstract speculation inspired by the same subject. In spite of its deliberately tendentious character—it was addressed to Franz Werfel, who a few years later tried to escape from "vagueness" through conversion—it embodies a striking truth and leads us to take a close look both at Freud's point of departure and at the curious movement that took him back to that point just before he died. For Freud's unique work—partaking as much of meditation as of research, of the novel as of science—does not develop in a continuous straight line, but describes an enormous circle around one and the same motif that is constantly reconsidered. Beginning with *The Interpretation of Dreams*, where the real person of Jakob Freud scarcely figures in the Oedipean drama inspired by his recent death but conceived as the constitutive factor of the human psyche at all times and places, the circle closes in *Moses and Monotheism* with a grandiose vision of the Jewish parricide, that is, a return to the very act whose horror Freud had long ago to surmount, but which he re-embraces on the eve of his death and now calls by its right name, considering it as the act that initiated an entire civilization.

II

THE TWO CULTURES

By one of those coincidences that posterity tends to regard as significant, Freud was born on May 6, 1856, three months after the death of Heinrich Heine, the Jewish poet, who since he was also German, Rhenish, and Protestant, Parisian at heart and Greek in spirit, may be said to have incarnated the confusion and instability of his generation. Thus at a time when the German Jews saw an acceptable future opening before them, but suffered all the more from the obstacles created by the prejudices and inertia of the "others," the future scientist seems to take up where the poet left off and to pursue on another terrain and by different means, the long struggle of the Jewish intellectual against everything that hampers the powers of reason and subjects him as well to an unworthy servitude.

Supposedly the German Jews had been emancipated since 1802, but in 1856 their actual rights varied from place to place and were nonexistent in localities where the population was openly hostile. Though the decree of 1791 promulgated by the French National Assembly [to grant full equality to all French Jews] and extended to the Germanic territories during the Napoleonic Wars remained on the statute books, it was so inadequately applied that during the first half of the century it had to be reaffirmed periodically by new decrees. The years 1802, 1808, and 1848 gave the German Jews hope of liberation from their humiliating medieval status; but each time their hopes were disappointed, for every decree, regardless of whether it confirmed the principle of equal rights for the whole country or only for certain zones, merely pointed up the impotence of the legislator to overcome the resistances aroused by the slightest sign of change.

The Jews of Germany and Central Europe, who—convinced as Moses Mendelssohn had been before them that it was no longer possible to "demand the rights of humanity without at the same time demanding their own"—had greeted the revolution of 1848 with enthusiasm and taken an active part in it, were obliged to recognize that the common struggle had brought them no great advantage. They would have to wait another twenty years before obtaining the full civic equality in which they placed all their hopes of emancipation. To be sure, when decrees to that effect were finally promulgated—1868 in Germany, 1869 in Austro-Hungary—Freud had not yet attained the age of the great decisions that commit a man for life. He was only a young student at a Vienna secondary school; but now this student, like all other students, could expect to study at the university without having to justify his presence or disavow his identity as a Jew.

In this respect the years of Freud's youth differed appreciably from the preceding period, when the theoretically emancipated Jewish intellectual had easy access to the prevailing culture but was still held in a state of social inferiority and denied employment regardless of his position in the intellectual elite. Unquestionably the situation had changed a good deal since the days of Moses Mendelssohn, who at one and the same time was Kant's friend, a philosopher esteemed by all as one of the most brilliant figures of the European Enlightenment, and Frederick II's *Leibjude*, subject to humiliating restrictions and dependent on the king even for his freedom of movement. But though less material, the difficulties facing Heine's generation of German Jews were no less malignant, and quite apart from the outward obstacles they still confronted, doubts, shame, remorse, and disavowals kept their inner lives in a state of permanent civil war. Neither the literary successes of the most gifted—and there was no lack of talent among them— nor the extraordinary influence of the Jewish salons of Berlin, which the Romantic Gentile intelligentsia frequented in search of stimulation, nor the revolutionary agitation in which some of the Jewish intellectuals engaged in the hope of liberating themselves and mankind at one stroke, could diminish the ravages of this internal civil war, for however celebrated a Germanized Jewish intellectual might be, he was by the very nature of his situation in perpetual conflict with himself. If he was to become a German, he had to destroy himself as a Jew in the name of something that he was not or not yet, or that he was only in his own eyes, and certainly not in the eyes of the community with which he aspired to merge. He could change his name, formally espouse Catholicism or Protestantism, adopt the tone and manners of the German intellectual élite, contribute by his talent to the glory of the German language—all that was counted for nothing and his efforts to pass unnoticed only attracted attention by emphasizing precisely the distinctive characteristics he wished people to forget, because regardless of whether they were judged to be interesting or suspect or repugnant, these characteristics were in themselves a cause of discrimination. The harder he worked to efface his singularity, the less the "others" were inclined to regard him as one of them, for everyone knows that a native requires no special effort to conform to his country's customs and habits of thought, whereas a foreigner gives himself away by his need to explain and understand not only complicated matters, but the simplest trifles, the thousand nothings that are said and done mechanically in every moment of daily life. The native, to whom all this is self-evident, instantly recognizes the outsider by the trouble he takes to explain the obvious, and by the naïveté which leads him to suppose that once everything is explained to him he will look and act so much like a native that no one will see the difference. Thus the Germanized Jew, identified as a Jew by the very effort which he hoped would make him unrecognizable, recognized for what he was but rejected in his claim to be the equal of his adoptive fellow citizens, was still in that half-tragic, half-grotesque, and entirely false position that Ludwig Börne characterized with such admirable succinctness: "It's a kind of miracle! I've experienced it a thousand times, and yet it still seems new to me. Some find fault with me for being a Jew; others forgive me; still others go so far as to compliment me for it; but every last one of them thinks of it. They seem caught in this magic circle of Jewishness; none of them can get out of it."[1]

Quite regardless of legislation, this state of affairs, described in 1832 with the lucidity and irony typical of German-Jewish literature, continued long after the beginnings of assimilation, as we can see from countless Jewish writings—letters, diaries, novels—which at the end of the century repeat the same plaint with the same astonishment. Half a century after the decree definitively granting the Jews equal rights, the surveyor, K., in Kafka's *Castle*, was still trying to break through the magic circle of Jewishness by becoming exactly like the natives among whom he had decided to settle: "Only as a worker in the village, removed as far as possible from the sphere of the Castle, could he hope to achieve anything in the Castle itself; the village folk, who were now so suspicious of him, would begin to talk to him once he was their fellow citizen, if not exactly their friend; and if he were to become indistinguishable from Gerstäcker or Lasemann—and that must happen as soon as possible, everything depended on that—then all kinds of paths would be thrown open to him, which would remain not only forever closed to him but quite invisible were he to depend merely on the favor of the gentlemen in the Castle . . ."[2] We know what became of this attempt at assimilation *from below*, of which Kafka dreamed as his last chance of shattering the magic spells of false resemblance and false identity: to become like the Gerstäckers and Lasemanns he first had to understand them; that is, since he was not a native and nothing was given to him gratis, he had to observe them incessantly, study their actions, their habits, the laws they seemed to observe, interpret their traditions, superstitions and legends *ad infinitum*. This intense intellectual activity referred him back to the impenetrable authorities of the Castle and wore him out; worst of all, it distinguished him from the natives more radically than the admission of his otherness would have done.

Since in the period of Freud's young manhood the question of equal rights had been settled juridically, for all time it was thought, the great problem confronting the Jewish intellectual was the twofold task to which Kafka's hero and Kafka himself were soon to succumb: to overcome the eternal hostility of the Gerstäckers and Lasemanns by making himself resemble them so closely as to pass unnoticed among them, but at the same time to stand aside and watch them live, to heap up observations and interpret them, rather in the manner of an ethnologist studying a native tribe at the antipodes of his own situation.[3] To display his oddity by trying to be the same as those around him: such was the situation, paradoxical to the point of absurdity, of the Vienna, Berlin, or Prague Jew once he had passed the first stages of Germanization. Like so many others, Freud had no need to decide whether or not he wanted to assume this role or whether he would be equal to it. Like it or not, there it was. We do not know how he felt about it in his schooldays or when he was choosing his career. But this much is certain: that unlike a good many writers and thinkers who found themselves in a comparable situation before and since, he did not experience his dual allegiance as a painful dilemma (not at least until the rise of Nazism, and after that there was no dilemma).[4] Such questions do not seem to have troubled him in the least. Apparently, he felt himself to be Jewish and German—more Jewish than German in Paris, for example, when a French revanchist took him to task,[5] but more German than Jewish in 1914 when the culture to which he was deeply attached seemed to be in danger[6]—and apparently this dual allegiance, which tormented others with doubts and feelings of guilt, left him unruffled. Apparently, I say, for in such matters one should not rely too much on appearances.

A Jew by birth, the son of a family still close to traditional Jewish life, though at least on his father's side open or half open to outside influences,[7] Freud naturally followed the path his father had traced for him by the mere fact of settling in Vienna. This Jakob Freud had done no doubt for economic reasons, probably with no clear idea of what living in Vienna would mean to his sons, in any case without being in any position to guide them. To judge by his son's reminiscences and a few meager documents, Jakob Freud must still have been very much an eastern European Jew both in his ways and in his appearance. The anecdote of the cap shows that in Freiberg, Moravia, where Jakob was living at the time of Sigmund's birth, a Christian passer-by could still identify him at a glance. This story, which Freud relates in *The Interpretation of Dreams*, moved him deeply as a child and was still a source of grief to him as a man in his forties. "I may have been ten or twelve years old," he writes, "when my father began to take me with him on his walks and reveal to me in his talk his views upon things in the world we live in. Thus it was, on one such occasion, that he told me a story to show me how much better things were now than they had been in his day. 'When I was a young man,' he said, 'I went for a walk one Sunday in the streets of your birthplace; I was well-dressed, and had a new fur cap on my head. A Christian came up to me and with a single blow knocked off my cap into the mud and shouted: 'Jew! get off the pavement!' 'And what did you do?' I asked. 'I went into the roadway and picked up my cap,' was his quiet reply."[8] In a letter to a correspondent who had questioned him about his religious antecedents, Freud writes: "It may interest you to hear that my father did indeed come from a Chassidic background. He was forty-one when I was born and had been estranged from his native environment for almost twenty years. My education was so un-Jewish that today I cannot even read your dedication, which is evidently written in Hebrew. In later life I have often regretted this lack in my education."[9]

Freud tells us nothing of the circumstances under which his father fell away from religion, nor do we know whether his ties with the synagogue were severed or merely slackened. In either case, it seems reasonable to suppose that he was in the situation characteristic of the recent transplant who according to Kafka was a source of painful problems to the younger generation. The father who cut his ties with tradition by moving to the city from a small rural community, preserved within himself enough living Judaism to save him from being dangerously uprooted, but, since all he could pass on to his children was snatches of folklore seasoned with humiliating memories, they were left with a dead past, an uncertain future, and a present that had to be created out of the whole cloth. Yet Freud's Jewish education cannot have been as utterly neglected as he claims in the above-cited letter, where, finding his correspondent somewhat importunate, he pretended to forget that he had studied Hebrew and Scripture at school, and that his teacher, Samuel Hammerschlag, far from being an episodic or insignificant figure in his childhood, later became one of his dearest friends and a mainstay in difficult moments.[10] He also neglects to mention the fact that on his thirty-fifth birthday his father had presented him with his own Bible with a dedication in Hebrew, which would have been absurd if its author had not known full well that it would be read and understood.[11] But quite apart from this singular lapse of memory, Jakob Freud was undoubtedly the transitional man whose development is summed up in his son's letter. He had taken a first decisive step away from the orthodox Judaism of his ancestors but had made no attempt to find a new spiritual home in which he and his children could sink roots. Thus he left the most gifted of his sons in an ambiguous position, halfway between the complete break with Judaism, that would have been logical and the full allegiance that was no longer possible.

Hostile or indifferent to religion as Freud's father may have become late in life, the Bible remained for him the embodiment of all culture. This we know from the book in which little Sigmund seems to have learned to read and which was given to him at the age of thirty-five as a pledge of his future intellectual success. At thirty-five, to be sure, Freud was not yet the inventor of a radically novel not to say scandalous science, but he already had considerable scientific accomplishments to his credit. He had worked in Paris and Berlin, translated a work by John Stuart Mill and a part of Charcot's *Leçons;* he had published several papers on pathology, and in that same year (1891) had ventured outside his special field with a study of aphasia. That was the moment chosen by his father, in accordance with a Central European tradition which dates a man's maturity from the age of thirty-five,[12] to give him a book which, quite apart from its value as a family relic and the tender memories it evoked, obviously retained much of its ancient majesty and virtue in the eyes of Jakob Freud. To his mind, the Bible was the secret guide and sponsor of this beloved son born to him on the threshold of old age; the Bible rather than any learned human teachers was responsible for his love of knowledge and the flowering of his genius. Was the father aware that such sponsorship was none too compatible with the young scientist's intellectual orientation or with his need for what he called the truth? Of this he has nothing to say, but the almost biblical words that he wrote in the flyleaf of the "Book of Books" clearly expresses his conviction that this doubly symbolic gift provided a bond between him and his son: "To my dear son Solomon: It was in the seventh year of your age that the spirit of God spoke to you thus: 'Read in My book. There will be opened to thee sources of knowledge and of the intellect.' It is the Book of Books; it is the well that wise men have digged and from which lawgivers have drawn the waters of their knowledge. You have seen in this Book the vision of the Almighty, you have heard willingly, you have acted and have tried to fly high upon the wings of the Holy Spirit. Since then I have preserved the same Bible. Now, on your thirty-fifth birthday I have brought it out of its retirement and I send it to you as a token of love from your old father."[13] Thus, though the old man may have moved away from the faith of his youth and even, as Freud tells us, renounced it altogether, the Bible remained for him the eternal source of wisdom; all study, he believed, has the Bible as its starting point; and the spirit of even the most profane science draws nourishment from it. It is indeed the Book of Books; in what other book could this father and this son have found an inviolable meeting place, a consecration as it were of the bond between them?

It seems reasonable to suppose that this Jew, so well able to combine religious indifference with fervent piety toward the Holy Scriptures, had taken only the timidest of steps toward Western culture. And such was indeed the case, as Freud—either directly or in accounts of his dreams—tells us at various points in his work. He also tells us that he was made unhappy by his father's lack of Western culture, so much so that for many years his own intellectual attainments inspired him with a sense of guilt. Strictly a man of the Bible, Jakob had little respect for other books, that is, to all intents and purposes, for the books of the Gentiles. In a dream which Freud was later to call the "dream of the botanical monograph," Sigmund sees the old man allowing him and his little sister to tear up a book and relates this memory rather oddly to his own passion for printed matter of all kinds. This quixotic passion, usually identified with higher things, did not meet with Jakob's approval and seems to have been a permanent source of friction if not of actual conflict during Sigmund's adolescence. ("When I was seventeen I had run up a largish amount at the bookseller's and had nothing to meet it with; and my father had scarcely taken it as an excuse that my inclinations might have chosen a worse outlet."[14]) Thus in the Freud family, "the Book" was a connecting link between the generations, whereas "books" in general were a source of conflict and aroused a strong sense of guilt in the future conqueror of the unconscious.

Freud felt guilty toward his father because his father, versed in Scripture but ignorant from the standpoint of Gentile society, remained far behind him, living in a narrow spiritual world where his son's bold aspirations and insatiable need for knowledge had neither place nor meaning. At the age of eighty, Freud told Romain Rolland—in an extraordinary letter that is a little masterpiece in its own right—of a strange incident that had occurred thirty years before on the occasion of his first visit to Athens, and to which analysis had thus far not provided him with the key. But the momentary sense of unreality that came over him at his first sight of the Acropolis ("so all this really *does* exist, just as we learnt at school!") is easily explained as a consequence of the highly ambivalent emotions always aroused in Freud by his pilgrimages to the sanctuaries of Western culture, to those sites which attracted him irresistibly but at the same time repelled him, because Jakob Freud had had neither the desire, nor the time, nor the power to force their gates: "It is not true that in my school days I ever doubted the real existence of Athens. I only doubted whether I should ever see Athens. It seemed to me beyond the realm of possibility that I should travel so far—that I should 'go such a long way.' This was linked up with the limitations and poverty of our conditions of life in my youth . . . That day on the Acropolis I might have said to my brother: 'Do you still remember how, when we were young, we used day after day to walk along the same streets on our way to school, and how every Sunday we used to go to the Prater or on some other excursion we knew so well? And now, here we are in Athens, and standing on the Acropolis! We really *have* gone a long way!' . . . It must be that a sense of guilt was attached to the satisfaction in having gone such a long way: there was something about it that was wrong, that from earliest times had been forbidden. . . . It seems as though the essence of success was to have got further than one's father, and as though to excel one's father was still something forbidden. As an addition to this generally valid motive there was a special factor present in our particular case. The very theme of Athens and the Acropolis in itself contained evidence of the son's superiority. Our father had been in business, he had no secondary education, and Athens could not have meant much to him. Thus what interfered with our enjoyment of the journey to Athens was a feeling of *filial piety*.[15] Superiority of the son; pride in having gone a long way without an already "arrived" father to help him; pride in having escaped the narrowness of his family environment; love and piety—late in the life Freud described this hodgepodge of feelings in the belief that it was still characteristic of his attitude as a man living in a hostile world. And perhaps to remind himself and others, shortly before his death, that he had created his work for, against, and with the ignorant father who may not have read Goethe and who certainly took no interest whatever in Rome or in Athens.

Thus while others had parents who were almost perfect models of assimilation, Freud was obliged to start as it were from scratch and to work quickly, speed being in his case the "key to the whole situation" (here, to be sure, there were plenty of precedents; ever since Moses Mendelssohn took his place among the leading lights of German culture, German-Jewish intellectuals had forged ahead with almost miraculous speed). Unlike Einstein, whose father Hermann was already a "real" German, an admirer of Bismarck[16] and fervent patriot, Freud was attached to the Jewish world by ties that he knew to be indestructible; though an atheist and from the standpoint of strict orthodoxy no Jew at all, it never occurred to him to secede from the community (as Einstein did in his youth), or to re-enter it. With a semi-westernized father and a mother who spoke broken German to the very end, he could hardly have subscribed to Walter Rathenau's sadly prophetic profession of faith: "Like our fathers, we wish to live and die in and for Germany. Let others build a kingdom in Palestine; for us Asia has no attraction."[17] Georg Brandes once wrote to a Zionist friend: "It is the Gentiles who have given you a sense of homelessness; if the Gentiles had never made you aware of a difference between them and yourself, I doubt whether a divergence in temperament would have made you feel one. As for me, the Danish language is my fatherland."[18] To this Freud would probably have replied that even if it were true that the Gentiles were solely to blame for his sense of being different, it had become a determining force and created a deep and solid bond between him and his people.

Those interested in proving Freud's essential Jewishness have cited various character traits, an assortment of likes and dislikes, an innate predisposition to analysis and casuistry, his inexhaustible stock of Jewish anecdotes and Bible quotations, a certain "characteristic" view of life—as though it were possible to base a typology on such disparate elements. True, Freud attached great importance to marriage and family life; he was proud of having so many children and, conforming to a time-honored Jewish tradition, regarded them as a pledge of immortality.[19] He had the same passion for knowledge and study as his Talmudic ancestors, and like them he had not only the courage of his convictions but also a keen interest in, and the utmost respect for, the humblest matters of daily life. He observed the traditional duty of a teacher to help his poorer students, and, though himself in difficult material circumstances, he contributed regularly to their maintenance, sometimes for years.[20] Endowed with a strict sense of morality, which he declared himself unable to account for, he set great store by self-discipline and reproached himself bitterly for his weaknesses—indulgence in tobacco, excessive love of books, passion for ancient art objects[21]—as though the puritanism of his ancestors remained in spite of everything his principal moral guide. His very prejudices showed that he belonged to a persecuted people, for liberal as he was in much of his thinking, his attitude toward the masses, whom he identified with the "low populace," the "profanum vulgus," reveals the instinctive distrust of those whom a long history has taught to fear the sudden fury of the mob, and his thinking was directly influenced by this typical defensive reaction.[22] All that is true but vague—and vague truth of this kind cannot withstand critical scrutiny. For after all, attachment to family life, puritanism, a taste for knowledge and analysis, and the practice of social solidarity are not exclusively Jewish; and the *La Psychologie des foules* (1895; translated, *The Crowd: A Study of the Popular Mind*, 1897), on the basis of which Freud established his own collective psychology, was not the work of a Jewish philosopher, but of Gustave Le Bon, whose confusion of masses and populace undoubtedly had causes very different from atavistic fear. Thus if we wish to understand Freud through the complex of feelings, ideas, habits, and tastes which created a vast network of common interests between him and what he always referred to as "his people," we shall do well to concentrate on what he himself, in his voluminous correspondence and in the directly autobiographical part of his work, said on the subject, either spontaneously or in reply to persons who asked where he stood.

Here the earliest of his letters in our possession—written on June 16, 1873, to a childhood friend—takes on an almost symbolic significance. In it he mentions his success in his first secondary-level examinations—most noteworthy for his mark in German—and the frequent visits to his parents of a certain Herr Bretholz and his nephew, who was a "sage": "He really is a sage"; Freud wrote: "I enjoyed him very much."[23] Thus at the age of seventeen, at a time when he had just chosen his future career (abandoning the idea of studying law in favor of medicine), Freud still believed in the possibility of being himself in all innocence, believed, in other words, that he could be a Jew, enthusiastic about a "sage" from Czernowitz, and at the same time "serve mankind"—this was the subject of his examination essay—as a scientist who had become a German both in language and in culture. He seems to have held this belief throughout his childhood, which was not so unreasonable at a time when liberalism was triumphant and when for the first time in Austro-Hungary there were Jewish cabinet ministers. In the sixties, an itinerant poet predicted to little Sigmund, then aged ten or twelve, that he would some day have a brilliant political career; the Freud family celebrated the inauguration of the "Bürgerministerium" (middle-class ministry) which included several Jews; and the idea that "every industrious Jewish schoolboy carried a Cabinet Minister's portfolio in his satchel" enjoyed a certain credit because it had some basis in reality.[24] In 1873, however, such ambitions had become chimerical, the liberals had been defeated, the "better times" in which Jakob Freud had rejoiced for his son's sake were over, and the rise of political anti-Semitism[25] gave promise of distinctly worse times. When, full of hope for the future and still glowing with the equality he had enjoyed at secondary school,[26] Freud went on to the university, anti-Semitic agitation, hitherto unknown in its organized form, had invaded the student organizations, and the Jewish students were obliged either to defend themselves or to live in isolation. Freud, who had regarded this abode of science as a temple of universality high above the common concerns of life, was scandalized to hear his fellow students talking of race and blood, all the more so because in the liberal circles he had frequented until then it was held that such things were impossible in the "enlightened" world of the late nineteenth century. The disillusionment of the youthful candidate for the "service of mankind" was the source of the bitterness and resentment expressed in the above-quoted passage from *My Life and Psychoanalysis*. ("Above all I found that I was expected to feel myself inferior and an alien because I was a Jew.") But Freud was not so badly hurt as to content himself with mulling over his injury. Rather than resign himself to picking his cap out of the mud, he made up his mind that he would never bow to the "compact majority," that he would make no secret of his Jewishness, but work as a Jew to widen the field of knowledge, and if necessary to revolutionize science by revealing a new truth in opposition to the all-powerful official science.

Yet despite Freud's rebellion against the cowardice and intellectual baseness of the Viennese students, it would be a mistake to suppose that his Jewish feeling resulted entirely from the artificial difference emphasized by the "others," as Georg Brandes and most of the German-Jewish partisans of unlimited assimilation supposed. Far from feeling negatively Jewish, he knew himself to be positively Jewish by virtue of a cast of mind which a contemporary, for want of a better explanation, attributed to a "convolution of the brain."[27] What at the age of seventeen he admired in the "sage from Czernowitz" was far from being a negative quality; on the contrary, he held it to be something specific to Jewish life, and in spite of everything that stood between him and this Jewish life he felt himself to be a part of it. True, Freud was never a theoretician or prophet of Judaism as he understood it, but he was attracted to a certain kind of Jewishness, which he described at least once with the precision of a professional observer and the more subtle gifts of a genuine writer. This description, which takes up a whole letter to Martha Bernays, is worth quoting at length, because it points up the aspect of Freud's Jewishness that has been most misunderstood. The letter was written in Hamburg, on July 23, 1882, and bears as an epigraph an approximate quotation from Lessing's *Nathan the Wise*. Freud was then twenty-six; he was not yet the kill-joy of whom it was later said that he "profaned the past, poisoned the present, and killed the future"; he was an experimental scientist, an out-and-out positivist, who brought to science all the devotion that he would have given to religion in earlier times, and had lost none of his faculty for enthusiasm and admiration. He hoped to be in a position to marry soon; he had just seen his intended, and before leaving Hamburg he wrote her an account of a meeting with an old Jewish shopkeeper, from whom he had ordered some monogrammed stationery. In the course of the long conversation, it turned out that the stationer was a faithful disciple of Isaac Bernays, the celebrated *haham*[28] of Hamburg, in whom Freud had a special reason for taking an interest, since he was his fiancée's grandfather.

The man from whom I ordered this despotic paper on Friday could supply it only on Sunday; "for on Saturday," said he, "we are not here, it is one of our ancient customs." (Oh, well I know that ancient custom!) ... On Sunday I saw him again. He was very proud of the elegance of the monogram, but he did not wish to treat me as a mere customer. ... I had to take a chair beside him while he questioned me as to where I had already been, and recommended me to this and that excursion: "I'd like to come along with you myself, but I am an old Jew, and just look at me." I looked. His beard was shaggy. "You were unable to get a shave yesterday?" "You know, of course, which Fast Day is upon us?" I knew all right. Just because years ago at this season (owing to a miscalculation) Jerusalem had been destroyed, I was to be prevented from speaking to my girl on the last day of my stay. But what's Hecuba to me? ... And the historians say that if Jerusalem had not been destroyed, we Jews would have perished like so many races before and after us. According to them, the invisible edifice of Jerusalem became possible only after the collapse of the original Temple. So, said my old Jew, nine days before Tisha B'Av[29] we deny ourselves every pleasure. We are here a number of men of the old school all of whom adhere to our religion without cutting ourselves off from life. We owe our education to one single man. ... He went on to recall the memories of his own youth, and traits of Nathan the Wise now began to appear in what he said. Bernays had been a quite extraordinary person and had taught religion with great imagination and humaneness. If someone just refused to believe anything—well, there was nothing to be done about him; but if someone demanded a reason for this or that which was looked upon as absurd, then he would step outside of the law and justify it for the unbeliever from there. ... My old Jew provided several more ingenious attempts of this kind to explain and support the Scriptures. I knew the method: the Holy Scriptures' claim to truth and obedience could not be supported in this way, there was no place for reform, only for revolution, but in this method of teaching lay enormous progress, a kind of education of mankind in Lessing's sense. Religion was no longer treated as a rigid dogma, it became an object of reflection for the satisfaction of cultivated artistic taste and of intensified logical efforts, and the teacher of Hamburg recommended it finally not because it happened to exist and had been declared holy, but because he was pleased by the deeper meaning which he found in it or which he projected into it. It was criticism, even though willfully manipulated and directed toward definite aims, but well suited to give his disciples the decisive direction which my old Jew was still following while I was fetching our monogram for the granddaughter of his master. His teacher, he continued, had been no ascetic. The Jew, he said, is the finest flower of mankind, and is made for enjoyment. Jews despise anyone who lacks the ability to enjoy. . . . The law commands the Jew to appreciate every pleasure, however small, to say grace over every fruit which makes him aware of the beautiful world in which it is grown. The Jew is made for joy and joy for the Jew. The teacher illustrated this by speaking of the degrees of joy corresponding to the various Holy Days. . . . A customer arrived and Nathan became a merchant again. . . . And as for us, this is what I believe: even if the form wherein the Jews were happy no longer offers us any shelter, something of the core, of the essence of this meaningful and life-affirming Judaism will not be absent from our home.[30]

Already remarkable for the way in which the art of the storyteller backs up the opinions of the pedagogue, this document is valuable as a statement of principle addressed to a fiancée, who having been reared in the aura of a glorious family tradition and subjected by her mother to the strictest orthodoxy, could obviously neither share nor even understand his ideas. To avoid all misunderstanding—though we know that at the last moment he was unable to avoid a conflict—he wished at the very outset to state his ideas on the thorny subject of religion, and what he stated was no random thought but the principle of the intellectual method that he would apply later on in his theory of illusion. The reform of Judaism, as conceived by Moses Mendelssohn, the living model for Lessing's "Wise Man," remained a pure illusion, because in such matters no reform but only revolution is possible. The religious illusion ingrained over the centuries cannot be attenuated by compromise; one must either go on being its victim or radically destroy it, as Freud would do one day by tracing, with an appropriate instrument, new frontiers between desire and reality. The Jewish reformers, however, did not confine themselves to perpetuating obsolete beliefs; they also practiced a method of teaching which was an "enormous progress, a kind of education of mankind in Lessing's sense," in short, the opening up of a rational pathway, at the end of which the student would have some chance of laying down his old burden of constraints and prejudices. Because it helped to save an illusion, the Haskalah was no more defensible than any other modern attempt to rejuvenate prehistoric thinking (Freud was to say elsewhere that he preferred the old catechism to such attempts at modernization); but in so far as it taught one to do justice to the "increasing demands of logic," it prepared the way for "our god Logos," the only godhead to whom the inventor of psychoanalysis was able and willing to sacrifice in exchange for a serious hope of progress. Between the writer of the letter to Martha and the author of *Totem and Taboo* and *The Future of an Illusion* agreement on this point was not yet complete: the former required only to find the key to dreams—and in particular the dream of salvation characteristic of revealed religions—to establish his critique on a scientific basis.

If Judaism was susceptible of reform in the sense of slow, rational progress, it was because the "mystical element" is fundamentally alien to the Jews and because the early struggles of Judaism against idolatry left it, unlike the great religion descended from it, with a deep-rooted hostility to superstition and irrationality. Freud's account of the old stationer already implies the "it is easier for us" of his letter exhorting Karl Abraham to be more indulgent toward Jung; and through its reference to "progress" it is directly related to the meditation on Michelangelo's "Moses," in which Freud expresses his veneration mingled with terror for the culture-hero of the Bible, who in his eyes was perhaps not so much a prophet as a great educator and champion of rationality. But the Judaism he here[31] envisages is worthy of respect not only because of its mission or potential mission as an upholder of reason in its battle against mythology and superstition, but also because it is timelessly imbued with meaning and with the joy of life and because it is wise (which for modern man can only mean: wary in its quest for truth).

On this point, however, a good many questions remain

unanswered. What precisely did Freud mean by this core and essence of Judaism which at the age of twenty-six he thought indispensable to his future home? How did he interpret the timeless meaning, the joy of life embodied by the Hamburg stationer? And above all, how did he expect to achieve these ideals in a family radically emancipated from religious faith and observances? Martha Bernays can have had no doubts about the "essence" her future husband spoke of, for in her family there had been not several ways of being a Jew but only one, which consisted precisely in the strict observance of the Jewish law. One would like to know how before and after marriage Freud set about bringing Martha around to his views and to what extent he succeeded. According to Ernest Jones, the only biographer with access to direct information on the subject, the first years of their engagement were troubled by religious disagreements, but then Martha Freud was won over to her husband's ideas. But if this is true, how did she manage to preserve the "Jewish core" that he had explicitly promised to retain? Of this Jones tells nothing,[32] and since those of Freud's letters that might throw light on the question have not been published, our knowledge reduces itself to a few points. But on the strength of these points we can form some idea of the Jewish element in Freud's life.

It is certain in any case that up to the publication of *The Interpretation of Dreams* and even for some time afterward Freud's intimate circle consisted almost exclusively of Jews; the only Gentiles he came into contact with were professors, fellow students, colleagues, and patients, and he did not make friends with any of them. It may be argued that this aloofness from the Gentile world was not necessarily a matter of deliberate choice, that he had no reason to seek friends among people whose contempt or hostility was known to him in advance, especially since they did not always keep their feelings to themselves and distressing incidents could be expected at any moment.[33] It is true that Freud had unpleasant experiences, first at the university and later in medical

circles, where anti-Semitism was rampant; still, in Vienna at
least, open hostility was by no means the rule; the relations
between Jews and non-Jews who worked together were tol-
erable, though not always devoid of animosity; the director
of the General Hospital, for example, sided with a Jew—Dr.
Koller, discoverer of the therapeutic qualities of cocaine—
against a Gentile surgeon who had called him a "Jewish
swine" and had his face slapped in return[34]; and the daughter of a well-known professor, who was not only a Gentile
but exceedingly wealthy to boot, married the son of a Jewish "peddler or *shammes*," a certain Dr. Moritz Kohn who
soon achieved considerable prominence.[35] In short, there were
a certain number of liberal Gentiles courageous enough to
oppose the rising tide of anti-Semitism (there must have
been a few of them in the entourage of Professor Nothnagel,
an eminent physician who was active in the struggle against
racism at the university and elsewhere); and there was nothing to prevent Freud from making friends with one of them.
Nor was he obliged to choose his wife in a family known
for its orthodoxy and proud of its "sages" and its past. Obviously, he liked to be with his own people; he felt at home in
the house of Samuel Hammerschlag, his old Hebrew teacher,
who cherished him as a son, and this Jewish family where
the "essence" was undoubtedly preserved, was to him a kind
of ideal.[36] The Breuers provided him with another model of
the home which he himself hoped to found; he admired
them and confided in them, just as he later confided in
Wilhelm Fliess, the man in whom he found the Jewish character most closely related to his own, whom for years he
spoke of as his "only public" and who continued to influence
his work long after the quarrel that put an end to their
friendship. Often he thought of leaving Vienna (for years he
made plans to emigrate to England, which he regarded as
the home par excellence of culture and freedom); he was
devoured by ambition and harbored secret thoughts of some
day conquering high society.[37] Yet in the end nothing could
tear him away from his native environment, the only one apparently where he felt close to his fellow men and capable

of being himself. Unlike many others who in similar situations develop a hatred for their companions in their half-voluntary, half-forced ghetto, Freud never attacked the Jews as such and was never irritated by them or ashamed of them; he always felt a kind of attraction or sympathy for them. "That you were Jews could only be agreeable to me," he wrote to the members of the B'nai B'rith,[38] which he joined at the time when he felt the most desperately isolated as a scientist (after 1895) in order to find a little of the understanding and human warmth the professional world denied him. Despite the annoyance caused him by the somewhat indiscreet conjectures of A. A. Roback, he ended one of his letters to the young writer "with the expression of that sympathy which your courageous defense of our people demands."[39] And after the death of David Eder, the English psychoanalyst, Freud wrote to his sister-in-law, Barbara Low: "We were both Jews and knew of each other that we carried this miraculous thing in common, which—inaccessible to any analysis so far—makes the Jew."[40] At the time when he wrote these lines—1936—the social ghetto of his beginnings was far behind him. He had devoted friends and followers all over the world, and had become correspondingly cosmopolitan in his ways. And during the darkest years in Jewish history he had written a book which many of his fellow Jews regarded as an insult to Judaism or even as a kind of disavowal. But deep down he had not changed: he remained and wished to remain a product of that "mysterious thing which makes the Jew" and of which he admittedly knew nothing except that he was indebted to it for the good and the bad, the sufferings and the joys, of his perilous adventure.

The mysterious thing "which makes the Jew" and is "inaccessible to any analysis"—including Freud's psychoanalysis—is manifested primarily in a certain quality of human relations: it is a common bond which cannot be expressed in words and requires no definition. Preserved in the course of a long history of which it is at once the cause and the effect, it expresses itself in vast numbers of sacred and profane, grandiose and commonplace *stories*, which interpret it according to the needs of each generation. In regard to what makes a man a Jew and attaches him to his people independently of his beliefs and opinions, Freud saw no substantial difference between the narratives of the Bible and the Talmud and the inexhaustible store of jokes in which the Jewish people satirize themselves. If there is any hierarchy among all these stories, it is, he felt, determined by the circumstances under which they are told. Whether sublime or comic, whether recounting a moment of history or an incident of everyday life, they are all colored by the mysterious something which makes the Jew and gives the most trivial incident of Jewish life a touch of eternity. This at least was Freud's feeling in the matter. In any case, it is striking to note that when writing about the more serious and more painful events of his life he drew on Jewish lore for his metaphors and illustrations, while in connection with more superficial occurrences he tended to draw on the fund of classical quotations that every educated German has at his disposal. Thus in 1897 when he was forced to admit that his theory that sufferers from hysteria had been seduced in early childhood was a mistake which had ruined several years of work and endangered his livelihood, he wrote to Wilhelm Fliess: "Certainly I shall not tell it in Gath, or publish it in the streets of Askelon—but between ourselves I have a feeling more of triumph than of defeat (which cannot be right)."[41] On completing a chapter of *The Interpretation of Dreams*, which had in a manner written itself, he wrote to Fliess: "It was all written by the unconscious, on the well-known principle of Itzig, the Sunday horseman. 'Itzig, where are you going?' 'Don't ask me, ask the horse.' "[42] When after a painful inner struggle he finally decided to publish *The Interpretation of Dreams* (because he was not rich enough to "keep to myself the finest—and probably the only lasting—discovery that I have made") he likened his situation to the dilemma of the rabbi and the cock[43]; and when he finally decided to override his last misgivings it was again with a Jewish story that he explained to Fliess how dissatisfied he was with his work and for that very reason in need of approval: "I have passed the first signatures for press and am sending them in tomorrow. Perhaps others will like it better than I do. 'I don't like it,' as Uncle Jonas would say."[44] His letters to Fliess are seasoned throughout with the joyful or biting anecdotes which flowed spontaneously from Freud's pen in the course of his self-analysis, as though his descent into his inner depths were best illustrated by their malice and pointed absurdity.[45] But forty years later, when the Vienna Psychoanalytical Society dissolved itself and advised its members to emigrate *en masse* as the only possible means of evading persecution, Freud tried to bolster up the courage of his disciples by recalling one of the most dramatic episodes of their common history: "After the destruction of the temple in Jerusalem by Titus, Rabbi Jochanan ben Zakkai asked for permission to open a school at Jabneh for the study of the Torah. We are going to do the same. We, after all, are accustomed to our history and tradition, and some of us by our personal experience, to being persecuted. . . ."[46] Thus on March 13, 1938, on the eve of the disaster which was to destroy his work in Austria and Germany for years, this "absolutely irreligious" Jew took up the tasks and struggles of his ancestors: he would go to Jabneh and see to it that there should be no interruption in the propagation of knowledge, which then as always was the only true defense against the ravages of barbarism.

Freud's personal relations with Jewish history and Jewish lore cannot serve as a yardstick by which to measure the range and depth of his Jewish knowledge, for they spring from a very different source than a mere taste for literary monuments, and owe nothing to work and erudition. Freud lived on terms of natural intimacy with the great figures of the Bible; they were so much part of his inner life that he felt himself to be by turns Joseph, Jacob, and Moses—Joseph because he too was an expert in the interpretation of dreams; Jacob, because in his old age his children took him, too, to Egypt[47]; and Moses because, in fighting for a "temporal conception of life and the conquest of magic thought, the rejection of mysticism,"[48] which according to him were the true message of Moses, he was in his own way continuing the lawgiver's work of liberation. Yet deep-seated as it may have been, and important as it remained for Freud to the end of his life, a poetic identification of this kind can hardly be compared with the knowledge that comes of careful study. In the eyes of a specialist in Jewish history and religion, Freud's biblical efforts savor at best of dilettantism, at worst of adventurous ignorance (we recall Martin Buber's severe criticism of *Moses and Monotheism*, which is assuredly an adventurous work, although Freud took the precaution of presenting it as a "novel"). What exactly did he know of ancient and modern Jewish literature? What had he read and to what extent had he assimilated his reading? Unfortunately we possess little information on the subject, just as in general we know little about the sources of his thinking. While it seems unlikely that Freud was one of those Jews who, as Kafka put it, "see the pages of the Bible turning over of their own accord," neither can we classify him among those who had no feeling for it at all. His memories of the Bible are precise and vivid, ready to surge up at the slightest provocation and give deeper meaning to the present. Indeed, what distinguishes him from the rationalist Jewish thinkers of the mid-nineteenth century, whose ideas he shares at least with regard to the mysticism and superstition that falsify thought,[49] is that his cult of the "god Logos" never barred him from a profound experience of the inspired primordial images.

Despite his very special kind of intimacy with his cultural heritage, or perhaps because of it and of his tendency to assimilate the past to his inner life, Freud took remarkably little interest in the various social, political, and intellectual movements that had so great an appeal for the Jews of his day. True, he was a member of B'nai B'rith and for many years attended the meetings of his "Jewish brothers" regularly (every other Tuesday in the period of his friendship with Fliess, as he tells us); later he was appointed to the board of the Hebrew University of Jerusalem, and here and there he lent his name to a committee of some kind,[50] but otherwise he participated in virtually no Jewish activity, and one might even be tempted to call his Jewishness a purely private affair, if that did not imply a certain hypocrisy. According to a saying that was current at the turn of the century, some people are "men out of doors and Jews at home." That was not true of Freud. He was a Jew everywhere. But private life as he understood it meant far more to him than public life. Not that he regarded private life as the inviolable sphere of bourgeois individuality; on the contrary, he held that it must be continually violated, because it is private life, the hidden realm of each individual's dreams and secret desires that reveals to analysis the gulf between the true motivations and the avowed aims of men's public utterances and actions. For Freudian theory, there is no opposition between private and public life; on the contrary, private life explains public life and shows that its actions and utterances, its works and commitments are not objectively determined, as was thought when nothing was known of the unconscious, but are psychic phenomena, daydreams which, despite their bearing on society and the real world, spring from the same infantile tendencies, the same selfish desires as all other productions of the psyche. Plausible, even reasonable as they may seem, these phantasms raised to the level of acts and ideas are never entirely valid in themselves; they are never entirely objective, but only seem so by virtue of a self-interested confusion between inside and outside, or, as Freud put it at an advanced stage of his theory, by virtue of a tenacious illusion. For the inventor of psychoanalysis, however, this primacy of the psychic phenomenon over everything it engenders in the visible world was not a mere point of doctrine but a fundamental truth, which decisively colored his whole outlook. Though in his youth he harbored certain ambitions in the realm of public life, the more he discovered about the human psyche, the less inclined he became to take sides or to give his *official* support to any cause whatever. The only cause he championed was psychoanalysis, not only because it was his own creation, but because he was convinced that psychoanalysis was indispensable to all other undertakings as a measure of their degree of reality.[51]

Even before his discoveries, to be sure, Freud took little interest in official movements. We learn only from his letters to Fliess how shaken he was by the Dreyfus case, and how unhappy he was about what he regarded as the degradation of France. Likewise, when Karl Lueger, the anti-Semitic agitator who had seduced the Viennese population with his demagogy, was finally installed as mayor after an election campaign of unprecedented bitterness (despite the personal opposition of the emperor and the decisions of the courts which had invalidated his election no less than five times) we know of Freud's indignation and sense of personal injury only from his letters to Fliess.[52] True, he reacted spontaneously to every outbreak of anti-Semitism, to every glaring instance of persecution, but unlike Einstein he did not wait for anti-Semitism to become a threat before turning again Jew, for he never stopped being one. He would never become an official standard bearer of Zionism, although there is reason to believe that he was more or less favorable to political Zionism.[53] As soon as the Hebrew University of Jerusalem was founded, he became a member of the board, and wrote in a letter that his correspondent's "assumption that this university is dear and important" to him was correct[54] (for a time he even hoped that a chair in psychoanalysis would be established and that it would be given to Max Eitingon, who had settled in Palestine in 1933, but on this point his hopes were disappointed).[55] And to an Italian author, who sent him a rather critical book on psychoanalysis, accompanied by a short essay on the Zionist question, he wrote with mingled sadness and enthusiasm: "While reading your important work on psychoanalysis I noticed with regret that you cannot accept our youthful science without great reservations. . . . But your brief pamphlet on the Zionist question I was able to read without any mixed feelings, with unreserved approval, and I was pleased to see with what sympathy, humaneness, and understanding you were able to choose your point of view concerning this matter which has been so distorted by human passions. I feel as though obliged to send you my personal thanks for it. I am not sure that your opinion, which looks upon psychoanalysis as a direct product of the Jewish mind, is correct, but if it is I wouldn't be ashamed. Although I have been alienated from the religion of my forebears for a long time, I have never lost the feeling of solidarity with my people and realize with satisfaction that you call yourself a pupil of a man of my race—the great Lombroso."[56]

If not for this letter, we might know nothing of Freud's attitude toward Zionism, since (perhaps because the problem was so "distorted by human passions") he never made any public statement on the subject or engaged in any public controversy. Yet though his interest in the Jewish homeland was neither militant nor public, it was deeply ingrained. He speaks of it with wonder, as though surprised to see how much it meant to him. "But to come back to you"—he wrote to Arnold Zweig in 1932 after Zweig's first trip to Palestine —"how strange this tragically mad land you have visited must have seemed to you. Just think, this strip of our motherland [*Muttererde*=the eastern Mediterranean matrix of Western civilization. Tr.] is connected with no other progress, no discovery or invention—the Phoenicians are said to have invented glass and the alphabet (both doubtful!), the island of Crete gave us Minoan art, Pergamon reminds us of parchment, Magnesia of the magnet and so on ad infinitum— but Palestine has never produced anything but religions, sacred frenzies, presumptuous attempts to overcome the outer world of appearance by means of the inner world of wishful thinking. And we hail from there (though one of us considers himself a German as well; the other does not); our forebears lived there for perhaps half or perhaps a whole millennium (but this too is just a perhaps) and it is impossible to say what heritage from this land we have taken over into our blood and nerves (as is mistakenly said)."[57] Here Freud is speaking not so much of the Promised Land as of the native land once inhabited by semi-legendary ancestors, less a pledge of the future than a question addressed to the mystery of the past. And yet we know that on at least one occasion he thought of returning to this land, whose heir he felt himself to be though he did not know exactly what it had bequeathed him. In a letter to the man whom he then regarded as the closest to him among his spiritual sons, he wrote: "Something in me rebels against the need to go on earning money which is never enough, and to go on resorting to the same psychological devices that for thirty years have enabled me to keep my balance despite my contempt for people and the detestable world. Strange secret yearnings rise up in me—perhaps from my ancestral heritage—for the East and the Mediterranean and for a life of quite another kind, belated infantile wishes, unfulfillable and incommensurate with reality, an indication perhaps that my ties with it are slackening. Instead of which—we shall meet on the prosaic soil of Berlin."[58] Thus at the age of sixty-six Freud gave free rein to his feelings of revolt at the hopeless falsity of his position. He was sick of Vienna and the West, sick even of the science which both enabled and compelled him to preserve a balance that went against his nature and was almost beyond his powers. But though he barely hinted at his secret nostalgia for the Jewish homeland, he stated very frankly what in that moment of fatigue he knew to be the cause of his unhappiness, namely, his contempt for the "detestable world" of "the others," in which, though he could hardly think of leaving it at that late date, he was neither able nor quite willing to feel truly at home.

Though Freud's feelings about the "other side" were less profound and therefore less complicated than his feelings about his own people, they were neither simple nor purely negative. He was not always as pessimistic as he seems to have been on that day in 1922 when he confessed his weariness and desire to escape from an execrable world, and moreover, the Gentile world was not a homogeneous whole that could be condemned *en bloc*. For far from reducing itself to the frivolous, commonplace people of Freud's Viennese present, of whose intellectual backwardness and moral baseness he was only too well aware, it also included the men and achievements of the past; it was the product of a language and a civilization with which a Western Jew, even when disinclined to regard them as his own, is so impregnated that he himself does not know how much of his thought and being he owes to them. Freud could not prevent those Viennese whom he despised for their intellectual flabbiness and their prejudices from speaking the same language as himself, and he loved and admired that language as much as if it had been the language of his ancestors, if not more so. This common language created other common possessions, a whole complex of habits and attitudes formed in childhood. Like it or not, Freud shared with his hosts everything his teachers taught him about nature and the world, everything he had read in the classic works from which they derived most of their ethical and aesthetic judgments. As a thinker and cultivated man literally made by their educational system and molded by their conceptions of the good, the true and the beautiful, he naturally tended to think as they did in the situations of everyday life, and in matters of the spirit he related to the same ideal. Though this did not make him their brother and friend, he nevertheless, like it or not, resembled them in many ways, and this no doubt attenuated his negative feelings and made them more ambivalent. He could not reject these people *en bloc,* when he shared so many words and so much experience with them; at the very most he could criticize those among them who, it seemed to him, betrayed their own values and proved unworthy of their heritage.

But before examining Freud's share in the heritage of the Gentiles—that is, by and large, in the humanist culture from which he derived his ethical, scientific, and esthetic ideals, we must consider one important point that can easily give rise to misunderstandings. That is Freud's lack of sympathy and understanding for "the people" as such, an idiosyncrasy which some writers, on the strength of spotty observation and traditional prejudices, have termed typically Jewish.

True, Freud's aversion for "the people" is well attested, but here we must ask what he meant by "people." For him the word had two distinct meanings, relating to two distinct spheres of experience. The one was an immediate self-evident reality; the other was remote and problematic since, inextricably bound up with the movements of history, it could be apprehended only through a complex interplay of contradictions and conflicts. The first—the Jewish people—was to Freud a living organism to which he belonged by birth, which he knew without effort and would have known even if he had forgotten it or lost all interest in its existence. Concerning the second—the German people or "the people" in general—he had only indirect information, insufficiently controlled images which, too blurred or too clear, at once abstract and charged with the obsessive memory of frenzied racial hatreds, little more than blind forces suddenly set in motion, anonymous crowds suddenly seized with delirious convulsions. Thus while the Jewish people was for Freud a familiar reality which, independently of all value judgments, reassured him by its warmth and familiarity, on the other side the notion of "people" had an occult, sinister ring; it was the Sphinx, the absent one, a visitation from the world of irrational darkness, terrifying when it makes its appearance on the scene of history.

This opposition, however, should not lead us to suppose that Freud lived immersed in Jewish popular life as it still existed in his time, at least in the Jewish communities of Eastern Europe. The Jewish "people" in this sense was known to him only through what was left of it in his family circle, first of all through his own parents, who remained more or less typical of the class they had sprung from.[59] Apart from an occasional "sage" of Czernowitz, his friends in Vienna were classless, that is, they were Jews from everywhere, whose German education had separated them from their people but who had not compensated elsewhere for this grave loss. Still, the popular element was not totally absent from his day-to-day experience; a vestige of it remained very much alive in him; and later, when this popular element had gone out of his life, he found it again in the anecdotes which he collected to amuse himself long before he thought of interpreting them and applying them to his theory. For these stories, which he cited so often as examples, are more than picturesque bits of folklore; they communicate what is most original and authentic in the Jewish people; indeed, they *are* the Jewish people, come to remind the uprooted intellectual of his recent origins. Deep down, Freud, the ambitious scientist determined to succeed and to impose his ideas on the Western world, felt no more sure of himself than the little Jew from Eastern Europe traveling without a ticket, who is kicked off the train at every stop, but hopes to reach Karlsbad nevertheless if only his "constitution can stand it."[60] To judge by Freud's letters to Fliess and by certain pages of *The Interpretation of Dreams*, Freud was often able to identify with the hero of these jokes, but even when he could not, he had a weakness for this shrewd anti-hero who in a few words can reveal all the ironies and evils of the world and society. For this reason he pays him homage, not only by quoting him in connection with humorous situations, but also by associating him with what he regarded as the most significant part of his own work.[61]

We have seen that Freud's attitude toward "the people" as such had nothing in common with his spontaneous affection for his own people, and shows no trace of the objectivity or neutrality demanded both by his ethical principles and the requirements of his profession. For reasons which were partly personal and partly historical, he saw "the people" in an entirely different perspective. On the one hand, the Jewish people, a body of individuals, full of life and warmth; on the other, "the people," an inert mass, a blind mob, a hotbed of violence, for which he could feel only revulsion and unreasoning fear. It would be no exaggeration to call Freud's fear of crowds a phobia, for it was not based on any real danger, and he seems to have expressed it from the start by an analogy which would provide him much later with the central idea of his observations on sociology, namely, an analogy between "the people" and the deeper strata of the human psyche. Between the masses and the unconscious he saw a connivance verging on complicity, which endangers the highest values of consciousness and the achievements of the individual. Like the unconscious, the masses know neither law nor restraint; they are a conglomeration of primitive instincts impervious to reason and without a sense of reality. Hence the fear they inspire in highly developed individuals. Interested only in the satisfaction of their passions, hence inaccessible to logic, "the people" embodied the night side of the human psyche and showed civilized man what terrors still lurked in his own barbaric depths.

Since they are a collective embodiment of the untamable, unconscious instincts, "the people," in Freud's view, are the same in all times and places, regardless of their language, country, national history, and even of their apparent level of civilization. In all times and places they are terrifying, certainly in Vienna when they abandon themselves to the seduction of a Lueger, but also in Berlin or Freiberg, and even in the best policed of the world's capitals, Paris, where beneath the surface of the most peaceful street scenes Freud seemed to sense imminent insurrection. Soon after his arrival in Paris in 1885 Freud went for a walk; on returning to his hotel he wrote to his future sister-in-law: "Suffice it to say that the city and its inhabitants strike me as uncanny; the people seem to me of a different species from ourselves; I feel they are all possessed of a thousand demons; instead of 'Monsieur' and 'Voilà l'Echo de Paris' I hear them yelling 'A la lanterne' and 'A bas' this man or that. I don't think they knew the meaning of shame or fear; the women no less than the men crowd round nudities as much as they do round corpses in the Morgue or the ghastly posters in the streets announcing a new novel in this or that newspaper and simultaneously showing a sample of its content. They are people given to psychical epidemics, historical mass convulsions, and they haven't changed since Victor Hugo wrote *Notre-Dame de Paris*."[62] Here of course Freud is half joking; but his fear of the people was real, and they often occupied his thoughts. Two years earlier he had written to Martha: "But now please forgive me if I quote myself; I remember something that occurred to me while watching a performance of *Carmen:* the mob gives vent to its appetites, and we deprive ourselves. We deprive ourselves in order to maintain our integrity, we economize in our health, our capacity for enjoyment, our emotions; we save ourselves for something, not knowing for what. And this habit of constant suppression of natural instincts gives us the quality of refinement . . . The poor people, the masses could not survive without their thick skins and their easy-going ways. Why should they take their relationships seriously when all the misfortune nature and society have in store threatens those they love? Why should they scorn the pleasure of the moment when no other awaits them? The poor are too helpless, too exposed, to behave like us. When I see people indulging themselves, disregarding all sense of moderation, I invariably think that this is their compensation for being a helpless target for all the taxes, epidemics, sicknesses, and evils of social institutions. I am not going to pursue this thought any further, but it would be easy to demonstrate how 'the people' judge, think, hope, and work in a manner utterly different from ourselves. There is a psychology of the common man which differs considerably from ours."[63] Here the picture is less one-sided; we feel Freud's customary generosity and his gift of identifying with the disinherited, the weak and the sick (a gift which the neurotic would later give him ample opportunity to exercise). Here "the people"—Freud himself puts them in quotes—no longer appear as fiends, with the grimacing features of the eternal rioter; instead they are represented as at once pleasure-loving and unhappy, avid for immediate pleasures because the cruelty of nature and the oppression of society deprive them of the higher things. This is the other face of the barbarism to which the common man is inexorably doomed, first by his position in the lowest rank of the social hierarchy, then by his rudimentary psychic organization which, limiting his horizon to the present moment, prevents him from conceiving voluntary privation as a means of achieving cultivation and refinement.

Freud says he is "not going to pursue" the subject any further, but clearly he thought about it a good deal, enough to give his ideas the weight and cohesion of an almost complete theory. And by one of those anticipations we have already mentioned, his remarks of 1883 concerning what distinguishes the elite from the common people provide the essentials of the theory he would formulate later on, when psychoanalysis had revealed the enormous role of the unconscious in the workings of the human mind, so providing a radically new approach to sociology. All civilization, it taught, is based on the repression of instincts; it demands that the individual sacrifice his immediate pleasures in exchange for future benefits that he cannot even be sure of; in short, it demands a partial or total renunciation of the greatest pleasures in life, and its greatness is proportional to the unnatural sacrifices made to it. True, a time would come when the study of neuroses would teach Freud that the grandeur of civilization also involves strange and grave psychic disorders. But even then the explanation he had evolved some fifteen years before in identifying "the people" with instinct would remain the keystone of his doctrine as stated in his studies of collective psychology and the problematic relations between the individual and society.

It may be argued that far from being original with Freud this identification of the people with nature and instinct was one of those traditional commonplaces that frightened the conservative or liberal bourgeoisie and at the same time justified their privileged position in their own eyes. Yet this is only partly true. Freud did indeed fear the people, but not for the same reasons as the bourgeoisie, and though he too thought them inferior, he recognized—as the typical bourgeois did not—that this inferiority was due as much to misfortune and oppression as to any innate defects. He himself had been poor for many years—so poor that the fear of destitution would haunt him all his life[64]—and consequently he knew that the hopeless misery of the lower classes cannot be likened to the passing financial difficulties of the bourgeois intellectual, nor did he subscribe to the comfortable bourgeois maxim that poverty debases only the weak and de-praved, while superior beings derive strength from adversity. For that Freud remembered his own humiliations too well, and there were times when he hated the bourgeoisie, espe-cially the newly rich, as intensely as if he suddenly saw them with the eyes of their enemies. On one and the same visit to Paris, the common people terrified him because behind every word he seemed to hear the rumblings of insurrection, while the smug bourgeoisie parading their luxury and their smartly dressed children on the Champs-Élysées made him feel like a revolutionary: "Elegant ladies walk here with expressions suggesting that they deny the existence in this world of any-one but themselves and their husbands . . . On the benches sit wet nurses feeding their babies, and nursemaids to whom the children dash screaming after they have had a quarrel. I couldn't help thinking of poor Mitzi and grew very, very furious and full of revolutionary thoughts."[65] Freud's rela-tions with the bourgeoisie were far from simple. He himself was a product of bourgeois culture, to which he was in-debted for much of what he loved, admired, and believed; but he never espoused their cause as a ruling class and never associated himself with their interests. Though he largely conformed to the customs of the bourgeoisie, he thought the world they had created "detestable." By and large, he was bourgeois in his tastes and revolutionary in his vision, re-spectful of bourgeois conventions but profoundly revolu-tionary in his emulation of the ancient prophets, which led him to fulminate against idolatry and falsehood, hypocrisy and social injustice. Psychoanalysis was a product of this contradiction: born of the humanist culture which at the turn of the century was the pride, strength, and supreme justification of the ruling class, it was nevertheless radically subversive, attacking the bourgeoisie in what had hitherto been its securest bastion, namely, the family, and so divest-ing it at one stroke of its "eternal" myths and of its respect-ability.

Even in his youth Freud had been aware of these two con-tradictory elements in his make-up, though he could not foresee how the stronger but less evident of the two would some day gain the upper hand. Speaking of the timidity that gave him so much trouble in his dealings with people, he wrote to Martha: "One would hardly guess it to look at me, but even at school I was always the bold oppositionist, always at hand when an extreme had to be defended and usually ready to atone for it. . . . You know what Breuer told me one evening? I was so moved by what he said that in return I disclosed the secret of our engagement. He told me he had discovered that hidden under the surface of timidity there lay in me an extremely daring and fearless human being. I had always thought so, but never dared tell anyone. I have often felt as though I had inherited all the defiance and all the passions with which our ancestors defended their Temple and could gladly sacrifice my life for one great moment in history."[66] Freud believed this immoderate, quixotic passion that came to him from the remote past and smoldered unknown to all beneath his mild exterior, this defiance of common sense and social convention and the world of things as they are, to be the source of all his creativeness, and that is why everything written about him by writers who failed to suspect its existence left him unsatisfied. To Stefan Zweig, who in his portrait of Freud overemphasizes his "petit-bourgeois correctness," Freud wrote: "The fellow is actually somewhat more complicated"[67]; and if he had dared, he would probably have said the same to Thomas Mann, who rather cavalierly characterized psychoanalysis as an offshoot of German Romanticism,[68] that handy explanation for everything under the sun. For despite the obvious difference between them, these two interpretations commit the same sin of omission; they both fail to mention Freud's Jewish spirit of revolt and Jewish passion for ideas. The conflict here is neither between freedom of thought and petit-bourgeois conformism, as Stefan Zweig claims, nor between classical rationalism and Romanticism as Thomas Mann supposes; it consists, rather, in an antinomy between the order to which an assimilated Jew aspired and the prophetic radicalism, rooted in the distant past, which impelled him to reject any compromise with established institutions. Thus Freud the eternal Jew was a revolutionary, while Freud the semi-bourgeoisified Jew of his time was a conservative; he was pusillanimous in so far as he had appropriated the ethical and intellectual norms of a borrowed culture; but rebellious and bold to the point of rashness in so far as he perpetuated the dream of an intractable people, jealously attached to its own ways and to what it regards as the truth.

As long as Freud was groping in search of a realm of science in which he would be able to innovate, the prophetic impulse that prevented him from compromising with the bourgeoisie had no opportunity to express itself; he was obliged to wait for the surprising combination of circumstances from which psychoanalysis would one day emerge to announce a new era in the history of thought. Freud himself did not appreciate the full extent of this madness, and thought it was counterbalanced by the classical spirit that governed his intellectual method.[69] Though he was prepared to "give his life for one great moment in history"— and proved it when the time came by staking his whole career on the interpretation of dreams, which from the standpoint of contemporary science was sheer madness—he was rational, orderly, and sober-minded in his day-to-day life, a man of the Enlightenment, conceiving progress as a slow, rational advance in knowledge. And with regard to knowledge he could forget the "mysterious something" that set him apart from "the others"; indeed, he shared their ideas sufficiently to feel entitled to a place in their "enlightened" republic.

And never did it occur to Freud that this place might be elsewhere than in the front rank. For in the society where he was fated to live and work, there were only two ways in which a Jew could escape humiliation: by making a great deal of money or by amassing enough knowledge to force general recognition. Since riches were beyond his grasp, his only hope lay in study; since he could not be first in birth or fortune, he would be first in intelligence. Already in second-

ary school he was as good as his word; for years he was at
the head of his class, and this, as he remarks in a letter
quoted above,[70] appreciably reduced his feelings of rebellion (as one might expect, for by excelling the Gentiles in
their own knowledge, he removed at least one of the motives
of his revolt). He learned so quickly and thoroughly that in
the end his second culture became, as much as his Jewish
culture if not more so, to be a rightful family possession.

Thus Freud may be said to exemplify a successful German
education (or more specifically a German education in the
Austrian Empire of his day, where the schooling was designed to knit a wide variety of populations together) with
all its advantages and drawbacks. Among the advantages we
must number thorough and extensive knowledge; a taste for
literature and the humanities, conceived not as a mere intellectual ornament but as a means of shaping the mind; and
finally, a certain cultural cosmopolitanism, which was only
natural in a region where so many different nationalities
were obliged to live side by side. Freud spoke or read five
modern languages, German, French, Italian, English, and
Spanish (his knowledge of Spanish long remained a mystery
to his friends; no one could figure out where or how he had
managed to learn it[71]); he read Latin and Greek, and the
classical authors were so much a part of him that quotations,
usually in the original, came to him spontaneously as he
wrote, and they are so apt that one would not think of accusing him of pedantry. German literature offered him unlimited pleasure (unlike philosophy, of which he confesses
ignorance; for years he even claimed that he had never read
Nietzsche, an assertion which his pupils, always eager to find
precedents for his psychology, quite mistakenly put down as
coquetry); he lived on terms of easy intimacy with Goethe,
Schiller, Heine, and Lessing—especially with Goethe; indeed, there is hardly a page of Freud's work, apart from his
purely theoretical writings, in which he does not honor him
with a quotation or at least an allusion. But his admirations
did not stop at language frontiers; everywhere he found
spiritual brothers; here and there he met with idols and

above them all a god, Shakespeare, to whom he regularly does homage in his writings. In short, the choice of his mentors and the depth and range of his knowledge made him exactly what a cultivated German and European of his time regarded as an accomplished man.

As for the defects in his vision, they were the direct consequence of the strict humanistic discipline which, with its extreme concentration on the values of the past, left its adepts almost totally blind to modern cultural developments. For Freud, as for those of his contemporaries who in certain respects remained good students all their lives, nothing was true or beautiful or worthy of interest that had not been certified in the remote or recent past by authorities thought to be infallible; everything else was false, ugly, bad, or even shameful; only a vulgar mind could be taken in by such things, a man of refinement could never be duped by the falsehood or madness of "decadent" art.[72] As usual, classicism tended to degenerate into conventionality and academicism, but here more than elsewhere, for reasons rooted chiefly in the local situation, it engendered an enormous overestimation of culture and so became the mainstay of an ideology. Freud, who did more than any other man of his time to free the human mind from its inveterate superstitions, remained a prisoner as long as he lived both to the narrowness of humanistic culture and to superstitious enthusiasms, which in some measure compensated for this narrowness.

For years at the head of his class, he was the brilliant product of a curriculum which, heavy as it might seem to those of us whose schooling has been less rigorous, seemed expressly designed to favor his talents. Unfortunately, we have no direct information about the program of the Viennese secondary schools in the 1860s, but the curriculum of the German Gymnasium of Prague some thirty years later has come down to us, and this gives us a pretty good idea.[73] In 1893, for example, the first-year students (there were six classes) had eight hours of Latin a week; in the fourth year they took up Greek and Latin was reduced to one hour a day. According to the figures published by Klaus Wagenbach,[74] Latin and Greek took up a third of the school day in the lower classes; from the fourth class on half the time was devoted to them, far more than to German (first four hours, then three). The great philologist Fritz Mauthner—the same who spoke of Jewishness as of a mere "convolution of the brain"[75]—wrote that this cramming with the humanities, far from shaping the mind, merely deadened it: "They kept telling us that the study of Greek and Latin would enable us to penetrate the spirit of the ancient world, and that without that spirit it was impossible to acquire a modern education . . . The best students may acquire some inkling of the spirit of antiquity during their university years. Among us schoolboys—there were about forty of us in my class—only three or four advanced to the point of being barely able to translate one of the old classics word for word; this elite developed a certain conventional enthusiasm for Homer and Sophocles, but were utterly lacking in any understanding for the special character of the ancient spirit, for what makes it incomparable, inimitable, and therefore foreign."[76] The situation in Freud's day must have been similar to that described by Mauthner; if anything the program may have been somewhat heavier. By and large the same system was in force throughout central and eastern Europe. In Russia, Trotsky tells us, humanistic force-feeding was used deliberately as a means of curbing the spirit.[77] By the turn of the century, the value of classical education was beginning to be questioned; social critics declared the ideal it transmitted to be false or stigmatized it as a means employed by the ruling class to provide themselves with a docile bureaucracy.[78] There is no evidence that Freud ever expressed such criticism; on the contrary, he was grateful all his life for the education that had been given him, as we learn indirectly through various aspects of his work, and directly in a short piece on "Schoolboy Psychology," written on the threshold of old age as a homage to his revered teachers: "It gives you a queer feeling if, late in life, you are ordered once again to write a school essay. But you obey automatically, like the old soldier who at the word 'Attention!' cannot help dropping whatever he may have had in his hands and who finds his little fingers pressed along the seams of his trousers. It is strange how readily you obey such an order, as though nothing in particular had happened in the last half-century. But in fact you have grown old in the interval, you are on the eve of your sixtieth birthday . . . As little as ten years ago, perhaps, you may have had moments at which you suddenly felt quite young again . . . At such moments as these, I used to find, the present time seemed to sink into obscurity and the years between ten and eighteen would rise from the corners of my memory, with all their intuitions and illusions, their painful distortions and heartening successes—my first glimpses of an extinct civilization (which in my case was to bring me as much consolation as anything else in the struggles of life), and my first contacts with the sciences (it seemed to me that I would be quite free to choose to which of them I would dedicate what I had no doubt would be my inestimable services). I seem to remember that through the whole of this time there ran a premonition of a task ahead, till it found public expression in my valedictory essay as a wish that I might in the course of my life contribute something to our human knowledge."[79] As we see, Freud had no recollection of having suffered from the severe intellectual discipline of his childhood, but felt it had given him lifelong consolation; far from complaining of the forced humanism which so many others found crushing, he was convinced that it had made him what he was, that his education had molded his mind and character, so fulfilling the claims of the official doctrine. He remembered with emotion that he was proud of the men who taught him "the culture of the past . . . of their knowledge and spirit of justice."[80] He had turned the world upside down by revealing the impure source of all the creations of the spirit, and yet it never occurred to him for one moment to find fault with his old teachers for the wrongness of their teaching methods or for their blind faith in a supposedly eternal, and for that very reason false, ideal. For this ideal remained his as long as he lived; in this respect

he never changed; to the end of his life he believed in classical antiquity as the source of all wisdom and all truth, as the
supreme pledge of humanity, the only one indeed that was
worth defending, even against the profane methods and sacrilegious reductions that his science imposed on him.

Though it assumed unusual proportions in Freud,[81] this
cult of antiquity was not at all unusual at the time; it was
widespread among Germans and among assimilated Jews as
well, for it provided neutral ground on which the two could
meet. It was safer to discuss "immortal" truths than thorny
questions of religion and politics. No one was likely to question Homer's greatness, and it had the additional advantage
of providing a common bond among all those who had received a certain education. In this sense the dead past offered
present means of communication and could be said to have
universal value. The Jew who admired Plato, Sophocles, and
Virgil, who regarded them as undying models of humanity,
who could read them in the original and knew them well
enough to quote them aptly and with ease had provided
himself with an excellent means of approaching the Gentile
world without fear of being insulted and rebuffed; delivered
at least for the time being of his unfortunate particularity, he
was capable of becoming the equal if not the superior of any
member whatsoever of the intellectual ruling class (Hel-
lenists like Jacob Bernays and Fritz Mauthner proved that
Jews could be something more than dilettantes in "Gentile" humanism.[82] This neutralization of the "other side" by
the fetish of ancient learning offered the Jew an honorable
way out of his spiritual ghetto. A Jew whose profound understanding of literary works and monuments had made him
a citizen of ancient Greece or Rome could not hope for full
recognition as a German or Austrian; but up to a certain
point he could bring himself to believe that he had ceased to
be a Jew; above all, he could believe himself cured of the
aesthetic blind spot which is widely regarded as the congenital failing of the Jews, a shameful and degrading failing because it contrasted so glaringly with classical antiquity and
its legendary love of beauty. For generally speaking Jews

and non-Jews agree that the Jewish spirit stands in direct antithesis to the Greek spirit, because the Jews, forbidden by
an age-old law to make graven images, were excluded from
the world of art, in which the Greeks achieved immortality.
Thus to all the other misfortunes of Israel was added the
stigma of not being creative, which to an artist or poet is the
original sin. Heine embraced Hellenism as one embraces a
religion, in order to cleanse himself, individually at least, of
that unpardonable collective sin. Though he threw his whole
self into this conversion, it saved him no more than his other
conversion; and little by little, in an effort to escape the
painful conflict that his education had created, he returned
to the Bible which he now read with other eyes. "What a
great book! What strikes me as even more remarkable than
the content is the style, in which the word is in a sense a natural product like a tree, a flower, the sea, the stars, like man
himself. It flows, leaps, sparkles, smiles, one doesn't know
how, one doesn't know why, one finds it perfectly natural.
It's really the word of God, whereas other books bear witness only to the spirit of man. In Homer, the other great
book, the manner of telling is art, and though the content is
borrowed from reality as in the Bible, it is organized in poetic form, melted down, so to speak, in the crucible of the
human spirit . . . In the Bible there is no trace of art; it is
written in the style of a notebook, in which the absolute
spirit jots down the events of the day, seemingly without
the help of any human being . . ."[83] We see that even in this
fine passage with its enthusiasm for the Bible, Heine could
not give the name of art to what he himself characterized as
such—for what else but art would "a notebook in which the
absolute spirit jots down the events of the day" be? Nor
could he drop the conventional parallel with Homer, which
seemed to fascinate him. And then, as though the Bible's lack
of art had not been stressed enough, he dragged in the absolute spirit, in the belief, no doubt, that nothing less could
redeem the sin of an entire people against Beauty. The aesthetic shortcomings of Jewry continued to torment the poet,
and at the end of his life he was still seeking justification in

57

the idea of art for his return to the culture of his origins. Moses then became for him the unique artist who sculptured not stones but men, the great builder of human pyramids, whose beauty and perfection surpassed all the marvels of antiquity.[84]

There is no reason to suppose that Freud, who also devoted the last pages of his work to Moses, ever felt painfully torn between Jewish culture and the spirit of antiquity. Whatever consolation his intimacy with the Greeks may have given him in his struggle for life—which, as he tells us often enough, was in part a struggle to live as a Jew—he was never obsessed by the alternative which was a source of despair to Heine. On the contrary, he seems to have had no difficulty in reconciling the two cultures, in enjoying what both had to offer without drawing comparisons or exalting one above the other. From his point of view they were incommensurable: the difference between them was not a matter of art or philosophy, but of origin—one came from within, the other from outside. He could acquire Jewish culture without special effort, up to a certain point without reading or teachers, for it was part and parcel of the "mysterious thing that makes the Jew." It was something deep within him that he was in no danger of losing and that had no need to be found again with the help of pilgrimages and relics. It was so much a part of himself that he didn't even desire it. His position in regard to the other culture, the humanistic culture based essentially on classical antiquity, was a very different matter. Since he had to acquire it by discipline and work, it remained a second culture despite the importance it was later to assume for him; and because of its enormous scope it was bound to remain "superficial," that is, confined to the surface of consciousness, without roots in the deeper levels of the psyche. Whenever Freud's existence was threatened in any way, it was his Jewish stories that he cited; it was only in stereotyped, trivial situations that he quoted his classical authors, and what he quoted always came as a surprise to him, as though he could contemplate it only at the distance imposed by respect and by the magic of foreignness. We know that at least once he doubted the reality of this culture that had been taught him ("So all this really *does* exist, just as we learnt at school!")[85]; more often than not, in any case, he seemed to doubt that he had any legitimate part in it, and that was why he tried to reassure himself by collecting its relics and making pilgrimages to the two holy cities where his miracle had been manifested.[86]

Thus the two cultures which Freud combined, first in his private mythology and then in his work, were neither entirely complementary nor diametrically opposed. His attitude toward them varied with the freedom they left him, and in this respect the Jewish component was often the loser, because there his judgment was surer, more deeply motivated, and, paradoxically, freer to express itself. He never questioned the acquired culture to which his tastes as well as his intellect inclined, first no doubt because he was fascinated by it, but also perhaps because as a foreigner he felt that he had no right to judge it. It was very different with the culture he had inherited; it belonged to him, he knew it thoroughly, and was on terms of sufficient intimacy with it to speak freely. Thus the psychoanalytical critique is strangely reserved on the subject of Hellenism and seems to attribute almost all evil to Judaism as the first troublemaker, responsible not only for the neuroses of the individual, but for grave collective disorders as well (apart from its direct responsibility, it is indirectly responsible for the evils of Christianity, a doctrine based on the "repression of the instincts" and consequently disastrous to the health of the psyche). And yet, this apparent partiality is itself an indication that the culture which he criticized so severely played the more important part in his own inner dynamic. Spared the probe of psychoanalysis, the one culture remained on the reassuring surface of things as they should be, without any real relationship to the internal drama from which Freud derived his passionate thinking; while the other, partaking of the ambivalence of all true life, caught up in the endless circle of remorse and guilt, was the driving force behind his strange destiny.

III

AMBITION THWARTED

Jakob Freud, who was so glad to see Sigmund flying "high upon the wings of the Holy Spirit," did not live long enough to find out what part he himself would play in his son's most shocking discoveries. Yet there is no point in asking what he would have thought of them if he had lived to see them, for it was his death that gave Freud the violent shock from which psychoanalysis was to derive the heart of its doctrine and the best proof of its soundness.

It goes without saying that in 1896 when he suffered the common yet unique blow which his patients took as a real tragedy, as though no father had ever died a natural death, he did not foresee that it would give him an answer to the great psychological riddle that had been plaguing him for years. Though he knew only too well how the loss of a father could shatter the already precarious mental balance of his neurotic patients; though he was "deeply affected" in a hitherto unsuspected layer of his being,[1] he was far from suspecting the violence of the crisis that lay ahead or the enormous impetus it would give to his investigations. A growing malaise, psychic and somatic disorders similar to those he had discovered in his patients, and a disturbing slackening of his intellectual energies soon alerted him to the remote causes of his crisis; but it was not until he resolved to analyze his dreams systematically in the twofold intention of getting to the bottom of his own illness and of rescuing his work, which seemed to have run aground, that he fully understood what his father's death meant to him.

Freud could easily delude himself about the cause of the malaise from which he had been suffering for years but which had recently become much more acute, for he had only too many reasons to feel tired, anxious, and depressed. After having put high hopes in his new method of treatment —first termed the "Breuer-Freud" then the "free association" method—supplemented by hypnotism and the laying on of hands, he was forced to admit that he was not getting true cures; undeniably his patients had improved, but they were not cured, and worse, he was unable to determine where the difficulty lay—whether in his diagnosis or in his therapeutic method. He was losing patients by the day, his material security was threatened, years of effort seemed to have ended in failure, and how humiliating it was to have to cut back on his scientific claims at the very moment when his great discovery—the role of sexuality in the etiology of neuroses— seemed at last to justify them. Yet, though embittered, humiliated, fearing for his future and the welfare of his family, exasperated with his recalcitrant patients, but at the same time tormented with guilt at the thought that like a charlatan he was taking their money for cures that he could not guarantee, he never for one moment considered retreat. On the contrary, he persisted in penetrating more and more deeply into the unknown continents to which his neurotics had led him more or less in spite of himself; and instead of abandoning the method that seemed responsible for his failures, as might have seemed reasonable, he decided to put his theory to the test and if possible throw light on the mistakes that were interfering with its application by applying it rigorously to his own case. Encouraged to speak freely, his patients had led him to suspect the enormous importance of dreams as guides to the unconscious functioning of the psyche, which when analyzed threw light on all manner of psychic phenomena, both healthy and pathological. Very well, he too would keep a careful record of his dreams and then submit them to the special form of analysis he had developed little by little, in part by ingenious deduction, and in part with the help of his "brilliant" hysteria cases. The first dream he analyzed in this way—the famous dream "of the injection given to Irma," which would supply the dominant theme, the leitmotiv as it were of the *Traumdeutung*[2] (*The Interpretation of Dreams*)—did not, to be sure, bring a complete solution to his problems of the moment; continued analysis and a good deal of exploration was still needed; but it provided striking confirmation of his fundamental hypothesis regarding the significance of dreams and so justified his stubborn persistence in a method that seemed to lead nowhere, to defy common sense, and to go counter to his own interests.

The Irma[3] dream, when decoded with the help of spontaneous associations released by fragments of the dream text taken one by one, was to throw a bright light on the suffering, the dissatisfaction with himself and others, the envy and resentment experienced by Freud at a time when he saw his ambitions thwarted. Moreover, the decoding itself amounted to a beginning of recovery, for on the one hand it raised the dreamer above the petty feelings he was forced to acknowledge, and on the other it gave promise of the great discovery which Freud had never ceased to anticipate. Thus analysis confirmed the existence of emotions that the dreamer had long known from experience, but whose elemental, massive, violent character, out of all proportion to the place he consciously assigned to them in his make-up, he only now began to suspect. This confirmation of life by dreams would soon have enormous consequences; for the present it provided Freud with solid proof that there is meaning in the most absurd of dreams and that, once understood, such dreams can fully explain what the most sincere and well-directed introspection cannot help leaving in the dark.

To avoid all misunderstanding, however, Freud was careful to inform the reader that he would not publish everything he discovered about himself in the course of his strange adventure; that he would deliberately confine himself to a partial account, reserving the right to exclude matters that he judged too personal or compromising, that is, more or less, everything pertaining directly to his love life and sex life.[4] And indeed he breaks off his interpretation whenever it seems to be leading to a direct confrontation with this delicate subject—which is often the case, for, as he soon discovered, the essential function of dreams is to give veiled expression to hidden desires, and that makes them the best possible key to the dreamer's repressed and in some measure unavowable thoughts and emotions. Thus censored in advance, the published text may be said to continue the work of the dreams it studies: what is said negates what is left unsaid, so that the essential in Freud's hidden life seems to be not sexuality but desperate, unscrupulous ambition, the desire to succeed at all costs, to make a name for himself, to achieve immortality thanks to an epoch-making discovery. If the book is regarded as autobiography, this overemphasis on ambition at the expense of sexuality is of course a distortion, but at the same time it corrects the autobiographical picture in an aspect that is more important for our purposes, for in choosing to admit his ambition rather than initiate the reader into his private life, Freud was obliged to give an almost straightforward account of his efforts to reconcile his unswerving loyalty to the Jewish people with the disavowal implied by his desire to succeed by conquering the Gentile world.

Freud cannot have been too happy about omitting from his *Traumdeutung* what hard-won experience had shown him to be the essential; quite obviously he did so under constraint, for reasons that touch very closely on the character of the man who asserted the scandalous primacy of sexuality in human affairs and which also have to do with the recriminations and accusations that he expected from his contemporaries.

Indeed, Freud had no inclination whatever to play the role of the agitator and revolutionist that would be attributed to him when his discoveries were published. On the contrary, everything in his nature argued against it, for he was doubly a puritan: on the one hand as a man reared in an artificial society, whose morality consisted almost exclusively in sexual etiquette, and on the other hand as a Jew who had inherited, and in part retained, the traditional morality of his ancestors. We have plenty of evidence for this trait of his

66

personality, but the most direct is supplied by the letters to Martha, which are as eloquent in their omissions as in the preoccupations to which they constantly return. In these letters Freud shows himself to be a passionate fiancé, but an exceptionally chaste one, who never uses a word more daring than "kiss." Though the girl he loved was hardly an innocent schoolgirl, he kept close watch over her reading, and forbade her to see a girl friend whose reputation, it seemed to him, had been compromised, or to travel without a chaperon. Yet in all that there was no hypocrisy; in striking contrast to all those of his contemporaries who preached the strictest morality but practiced nothing of the kind, he observed his moral principles without apparent effort, and even after the logic of his doctrine led him to demand greater sexual freedom for his fellow men, made no change in the conduct of his own life. His thinking on the subject progressed more quickly than his ways, and in his mature years he wrote, perhaps not without a note of regret, that he personally had not benefited by the sexual freedom he had championed.[5] Thus his character would seem to account for his discretion, not only in sexual matters but even more so concerning his sentimental life, where he did not even feel the need to justify his silence, apparently preferring to give an impression of coldness rather than reveal his secrets.[6]

Yet he had still other reasons for hesitating to publish his discovery. At the time when he was asking himself whether to make public what he had learned from dreams or to keep silent—the dilemma is in itself significant—he was forty, a married man with six children and heavy responsibilities; the pattern of his life had been marked out and he had neither the desire nor the power to change it. His self-analysis was in itself a risky enough adventure; he could reasonably expect certain advantages from it, increased self-knowledge, an improvement of his psychic condition, and the consolation of seeing his theories confirmed by a radically new kind of experiment; but good sense forbade him to hope that it would give him a new personality, with different tastes, different ethical principles, a different sensibility. Thus he had to reckon with his existing likes and dislikes, for he had no substitute system of morality whereby to change them. Such, no doubt, were the thoughts that led him to publish his *Traumdeutung*, at the risk of being regarded as "the one villain among all the sterling characters who inhabit the earth" and to expose his name to the unhealthy curiosity of the public. If it was necessary to take the step, then at least he would do it in such a way as to incur as little injury as possible and to safeguard the privacy of his family.[7] He therefore gave notice that he would not say everything, and not the "best" of what he knew. But what he kept to himself falsified his confession by leading him to overemphasize, perhaps more than he would have liked, the only weaknesses and "villainies" that his moral code left him free to speak of.

Of course this compromise can also be explained by the need to spare the sensibilities of a prudish public and to avoid the recriminations of more or less well-meaning colleagues who had sexual theories of their own but were careful to expound them only in private. Still, this obstacle was not as massive as Freud supposed (he ignored it in his ensuing works), or rather, it was more complex. For the prudery of the period applied not so much to sex itself as to how one spoke of it: it was perfectly permissible to speak of sex as a vice, to study its perversions and disorders, to treat it as an object of scientific observation[8]; what was not permissible was to consider it in detail, in its day-to-day reality, as Freud was obliged to do by the very nature of his work; that was to invite accusations of pornography. To speak of such things was thought shocking[9]; yet no one was scandalized at the blackness that Freud found deep in his dreams: the passionate ambition, the secret desire to eliminate his rivals and competitors, the drive to be first in everything, were not judged very severely by a society that does everything it can to favor such strivings. Thus, as Freud wrote to Fliess, he was able to avoid sex but not "dirt," which he regarded as "unavoidable"[10]; his contemporaries were far less troubled by this dirt than by the few sexual improprieties that he could not help letting slip through.[11]

Thus everything contributed to magnifying the "villainy" of which Freud felt guilty in his hard struggle to achieve a place worthy of him; but of course neither his natural prudishness nor his vestigial prejudices nor even his fear of alienating public opinion would have sufficed to cause such a shift of emphasis if ambition, which was indeed a dominant trait in his character, had not been a constant cause of suffering and disappointment in the dark years preceding the *Traumdeutung.* True, by the age of forty Freud had done outstanding work as a physician and researcher; he had published noteworthy papers in the fields of pathology and neurology, had made a name for himself among specialists, and had built up a practice sufficient to keep him and his family. But he had not yet done anything to draw the attention of wider scientific circles; he had not yet made the sensational discovery which he had always counted on and in comparison with which his relative successes struck him as deplorable failures. And to make matters worse, he had narrowly missed two occasions to win glory: once in 1882 when he hit on the essence of the neuron theory but neglected to formulate his discovery, and again in 1884 when he dropped his investigations of cocaine before discovering the principle of local anesthesia, which brought fame to his friend Koller.[12] Since then he had made some discoveries that were far from negligible; after improving Breuer's cathartic method, he had identified the mechanisms of resistance and transfer that play a determining role in this treatment; he had extended the theory of specific defense suggested to him by hysteria to all the psychoneuroses, and discovered the "physiological expressions of repressed ideas" in the symptoms of hysteria; he had even progressed to the point of asserting the sexual etiology of hysteria and perhaps of all the disorders that he grouped under the head of psychoneuroses. But none of these discoveries was firmly established; they were far from forming a coherent whole; they had all been arrived at by an empirical method that could hardly be expected to yield shattering revelations; and his latest discovery, on which he was prepared to stake his reputation, had caused a permanent break with Breuer, his mentor and friend, a man of integrity in whom he had unlimited confidence.[13] In 1895, the year in which for the first time he analyzed one of his own dreams, he had reason to feel that he was further than ever from the glory he coveted; Breuer's disavowal left him alone, morally at sea, tormented by doubts as to the value of his work, and terrified at the thought that he might be on the wrong track. If only his patients had brought him a little consolation, but it almost seemed as though they didn't want to recover, and many deserted him for no reason he could fathom. To complete his humiliation, he had not yet acquired the title of Professor Extraordinarius, the indispensable badge of success for a scientist in Vienna, and was still a *Privatdozent*. Thus it should not surprise us that his dreams reveal much less sexuality than ambition—a "villainous" careerism that would stop at nothing to achieve success. The ideas of grandeur that had always been with him, now exacerbated by frustration, obsessed him day and night, in his waking thoughts and in his dreams. Yet by an irony of fate, which he may have begun to suspect, the analysis of his dreams of ambition would open the gates of fame, which his more "serious" works had been unable to force.

It may not be immediately apparent to a present-day reader of the *Traumdeutung* that ambition is the central motive in those of his own dreams that Freud analyzes, because in the course of writing he included a large number of other people's dreams—mostly provided by the first generation of his pupils—and lost among them his own dreams lose much of their relief. It was quite clear, however, to Wilhelm Fliess, the book's first reader and first critic, to whom Freud sent accounts of his dreams as the work proceeded. In sending him the second chapter with a request for advice and criticism, Freud promised an explanation of his "villainy," for he was beginning to fear that he had made too much of it: "I hope you will not object to the candid remarks in the professor-dream.[14] The Philistines here will rejoice at the opportunity to say that I have put myself beyond the pale. The thing in the dream which will probably strike you must be explained later (my ambition)."[15]

We do not know if Freud did this explaining by word of mouth at one of his conferences with Fliess; in any case, there is no such explanation in the letters; the only word of explanation occurs in a passage in the *Traumdeutung*, where he imputes the glaring cynicism of his dream fantasies, not to the careerism of which the Philistines would be only too glad to accuse him, but to a long surmounted infantile megalomania: "If it was indeed true that my craving to be addressed by a different title was as strong as all that, it showed a psychological ambition which I did not recognize in myself and which I believed was alien to me. I could not tell how other people who believed they knew me would judge me in this respect. It might be that I was really ambitious; but if so, my ambition had long ago been transferred to objects quite other than the title and rank of professor extraordinarius."[16] From the point of view of psychology, which always tends to discover an infantile element in present phenomena, this explanation is undoubtedly correct, though Freud's statement of it is not very convincing ("I have no ambition to be a professor; I have this ambition only in dreams, because in my childhood I wanted to be a cabinet minister"). But it does not square at all with Freud's other letters to Fliess, which are full of his desire to gain prominence at all costs, if need be with the help of a title and a rank which he secretly judged to be very much beneath his dignity.

What is most striking in the dream samples that Fliess received between 1896 and 1900 was the theme of ambition, repeatedly frustrated and as frequently revived, an obsessive theme which Freud forthrightly if reluctantly confesses, but whose implications—repressed violence, envy, etc.—he then proceeded to tone down for the benefit of his public. Alone with Fliess, Freud admitted that he was possessed by the kind of ambition which in addressing his readers he terms pathological and claims to be devoid of (elsewhere he justified it by his situation, since in Vienna a scientist could not be said to exist without an academic title). By "pathological" he meant of course the excess of passion that accompanies the pursuit of fame, not the pursuit itself, which indeed had nothing chimerical about it. Even considering the special difficulties created by his Jewish origins, Freud could reasonably hope to attain the high rank in which he saw the crowning of his career. Even as a Jew he could reasonably aim high, provided he was willing to undergo and to surmount the additional trials to which his false situation exposed him. In 1896 he did not yet feel ready to do so, nor did he then realize why not. He did not begin to understand what was wrong with him until the following year, when he threw himself into his self-analysis which, among other salutary effects, would finally give him the will and the means to take his dreams seriously.

For in the Austria of his day the situation was not such as to condemn his ambitions in advance, as one is led to suppose by certain authors who represent him as a pariah, exposed defenseless to all manner of persecutions.[17] Theoretically the Jews enjoyed equal rights; theoretically every career was open to them, though in practice there were certain restrictions—e.g., in particular, the army and the high administration were closed to them. Many Jews had achieved striking success, and some, without being converted, had even won official honors and positions. Since this situation is often misrepresented because of a tendency to see the mid-nineteenth century in the light of events that are much closer to us, it may be well to cite a historian who presents an unbiased view of the facts and puts us on our guard against anachronisms: "It has been suggested that the attachment of the Jews to the monarchy meant next to nothing; that they were pro-Austrian largely because they were not allowed to be anything else. In this there is some truth, but the whole truth is far more interesting, namely, that many Jews loved Austria and loved it for good reasons. When Franz-Josef was an archduke, there had been no Auschwitz. On the contrary, there were few countries in which the Jews had so many opportunities to escape from their narrow world if they wanted to. The transformation of Isaac Löw Hoffmann, silk merchant in Bohemia, to the factory owner and magnate Ritter von Hoffmannsthal [the writer's grandfather], had taken less than thirty years. At its best moments Austria was more than a tolerant state; it was truly cosmopolitan. Neither a halberd nor a unicorn figured in the coat-of-arms chosen by the nearly ennobled Hoffmannsthal; instead, it showed the leaf of a mulberry tree and the Tables of the Law. It was pleasant to live in Vienna."[18] Freud, who detested Vienna and its inhabitants, would hardly have subscribed to this judgment; but his hatred of the capital did not prevent him from loving the dual monarchy and expressing his loyalty at critical moments ("I have given all my libido to Austria-Hungary," he wrote to Sandor Ferenczi in August 1914.[19]) And Remak's contention that a Jew had a better chance of rising in the social scale in Austria than anywhere else is confirmed as much by Freud's dreams as by his conscious thoughts; the precipitous rise in life that figures so prominently in them was not the product of a disordered imagination and was entirely within the realm of possibility.

A case in point is the professorship that Freud dreamed of so often while working on the *Traumdeutung*. There were no official restrictions on the granting of professorships; Freud was as much entitled to the honor as any of his colleagues; he had only to make an application in due form.[20] The hitch was that at the time when he feared that he might remain a *Privatdozent* forever—he had been one since 1885—his colleagues at the Faculty of Medicine thought none too highly of his work (some even thought it "preposterous") and that the Minister of Education, Wilhelm von Härtel, an "old fox," whose anti-Semitic opinions were well known, always saw to it that Jewish candidates, while not rejected as Jews—that would have been illegal—were time and time again accidentally overlooked, until they grew sick of waiting and finally gave up applying. Of course Freud knew this; he also knew that in this system dominated by "pull," the minister's ill will did not necessarily have the last word, but could be neutralized by contrary influence. Yet between 1885 and 1897 Freud did nothing whatever to advance his cause; in January 1897 he informed Fliess that the Faculty Council had passed over him and appointed a colleague who was his junior in his specialty. This, he said, none too truthfully, left him utterly indifferent. A few days later, Professor Nothnagel told him under the seal of secrecy that he and Krafft-Ebing were going to propose his appointment, first to the Faculty Council, then directly to the minister if the Council were unfavorably disposed. Nothnagel had little hope: "You are aware of the other difficulties" (Von Härtel's anti-Semitism) and, to be sure, the intervention of the two celebrated physicians was in vain. If not for the importance this rejection assumed in the *Traumdeutung*, we would not know how keenly Freud suffered under the affront; but despite his bitterness, he still did nothing to counteract the minister's animosity, as he well might have, for four and a half years later, though the same Von Härtel was still in office, Freud finally obtained satisfaction by merely observing the rules of the game. In 1901—the *Traumdeutung* had been published the year before—he temporarily interrupted his self-analysis, overcame his strange inhibition about Rome, the model and symbol of several other difficulties, and asked Elise Gomperz, a former patient, to enlist the support of her husband Theodor, formerly a professor of philology and still a friend of Von Härtel; then he wrote to Nothnagel and to Krafft-Ebing, asking them to renew their plea. At first the minister turned a deaf ear ("Four years," he said. "And who is he?"), but another of Freud's patients managed to insinuate herself into his good graces and finally wrung the appointment from him, in exchange, to be sure, for a valuable painting (a Böcklin, it seems), which she gave him for the Modern Museum that was just being built. Shortly afterward, in March 1902, the newly appointed Professor Freud wrote joyfully to Fliess: "In the whole affair there is one person with very long ears, who was not sufficiently allowed for in your letter, and that is myself. If I had taken those few steps three years ago I should have been appointed three years earlier, and should have spared myself much. Others are just as clever, without having to go to Rome first . . ."[21] Thus Freud recognized that the minister's anti-Semitism was by no means the most serious obstacle, that he might have taken it as a goad to his ambition instead of remaining passive for so long. But before he could discover that the professorship was not as unattainable as he had supposed, he had to take a longer inner journey to the Rome of his dreams and also to set foot in the real Rome which until then had been forbidden him.

To understand this surprising association between the city and the title, both of which Freud desired and both of which escaped him for years, we must consider Rome as the highest symbol of the "other side," of the Gentile world to which he had been trying for so long to gain access by his hard work or better still by a dazzling intellectual achievement.[22] Rome was the embodiment of the humanist civilization in which the newly assimilated young Jew had sworn to play an eminent role, first as a political figure in the period when "every industrious Jewish schoolboy carried a Cabinet Minister's portfolio in his satchel," and later, when a political reaction had blasted that hope, as a scientist, since science, knowing neither frontiers nor discrimination, had the advantage of being open to all. After first choosing law—the Roman discipline par excellence—in order to become a statesman and to conquer the world after the manner of Cromwell,[23] Freud turned to medicine, in which he saw not so much a profession—from the start he had a profound aversion to the practice of medicine—as the privileged area where all-powerful science merges with and submits to philosophy. He would be not so much a physician as a scientist, a man of the laboratory, and thus fulfill the resolution he had taken at the age of seventeen to "contribute something to our human knowledge."[24] Indeed, he had gone into science as another man might have gone into religion, apparently without stopping to ask whether he could afford so costly a vocation.

He was drawn to science in general far more than to any

special branch of science; in any event, he was in no hurry to specialize, for every science fascinated him and none attracted him irresistibly; he let himself be seduced successively by the most varied disciplines, including some, such as chemistry and botany, for which he had no talent at all, and where his efforts came to nothing. To his mind, science was indivisible; the whole was present in all the parts; one could serve it anywhere, provided one did not lose sight of its first commandment, which was to recognize and communicate the truth. Convinced that science is reason itself and by definition transcends the ordinary limitations of thought, Freud passed from one discipline to another in disregard of the strict boundaries that the schools traced between them; on leaving Ernst Brücke's Institute of Physiology, where he had worked for six years as a pathologist, he became a neurologist, then a psychiatrist and psychotherapist, and if he had not in the end created a new specialty of his own, who knows what field of research might not have attracted him? But despite his highly professional conscience this dash of dilettantism so evident in his beginnings does not seem to have troubled him very much; he apparently accepted it as a normal counterpart to his unswerving faith in positive science, which he exalted as a universal authority.

As an embodiment of the humanist ideal, science soon became for Freud the strongest justification of "the other side," perhaps the only consideration that enabled him to confront an uncertain and humiliating present. In and through science he could hope to gain his proper place in the vast domain of knowledge, the place of a free man whom no one had a right to remind of his inferior condition or, more insidiously, of his duty as a foreigner toward his "tolerant" hosts. Science was not only the best means of serving knowledge by increasing the small stock of certainties with which man can fight against error and prejudice; it was above all the limitless field in which the titles and ranks that create such absurd dividing lines among men lose their meaning (Benedikt Stilling may have been only a poor, solitary doctor, unknown to the learned societies, but he was none the less the equal of the greatest). In sum, to Freud's mind, science in his day played the role formerly played by religion: it effaced inequalities, surmounted the barriers behind which individuals hide in their striving to dominate one another, and thus brings to modern man not salvation or a new golden age, but his only chance of working toward his own liberation.[25]

We recall Freud's disappointment when in his early days at the university he first became aware of the low moral and intellectual level to which this supposed temple of wisdom had fallen; but this did not detract from his idealization of science, which was further increased when he came into contact with a great scientist. Ernst Brücke, to whom he remained grateful to the end of his life for his encouragement and guidance and whom he admired perhaps more than anyone else in the world, came into Freud's life just when he was most needed to compensate for his disastrous first experience of academic life, for in Brücke he saw the scientist at his best, the inspired yet humble intellectual worker in his day-to-day reality. Uncompromising in matters of method,[26] with no patience for lazy approximations and premature conclusions, "terrifyingly" sharpsighted when it came to distinguishing the true from the false, Ernst Brücke was the living saint of the religion to which Freud had committed himself at the age of seventeen and which he would always believe he was serving, even when he was battling its orthodox tenets. But in a more prosaic sense, Brücke was also the "bridge" [German Brücke=bridge] by which the young disciple could legitimately cross to "the other side" and make a name for himself without disavowing his origins.

Of course the celebrated German who first brought rigorous scientific method to the Vienna Faculty of Medicine (his compatriots spoke of him in jest as their "ambassador to the Far East") was not alone in embodying the scientific ideal for Freud; there was Brücke's friend Hermann Helmholtz who as a physiologist and physicist worked with the same materialist ideas, and Brücke's two assistants at the Institute of Physiology, Sigmund von Exner and Ernst von Fleischl-Marxow, especially the latter, who to all Freud's other reasons for admiring him added the prestige of a hero-martyr.[27] Concerning Helmholtz, whom he regretted having missed on the occasion of Helmholtz's short stay in Vienna, Freud wrote to Martha: "He is one of my idols"; and even in his old age he spoke of Brücke, his master with the "terrifying blue eyes," as the greatest authority he had ever known. In Paris another prince of science, Charcot, took his place among the stars of Freud's scientific firmament, and Freud served him as an enthusiastic disciple, first by translating the Leçons into German and later by dedicating some of his finest pages to Charcot's memory. For Freud did not love science only as the abstract source of a disembodied knowledge; he loved it most of all through its great men.

Though science was above the contingencies of practical life, it played a practical part in Freud's life, for by providing a bridge between him and "the others," it offered him the surest if not the quickest means of making an honorable career. He not only admired such men as Brücke to the point of idolatry, as much for the passion they put into their work as for their inventive genius; he also revered them for the simplicity of their ways, their freedom from pedantry, and for the spirit of justice and freedom that are the mark of a true aristocracy. Brücke followed his pupil's work closely; often it was he who urged Freud to publish and who, one day when Freud presented him with what he believed to be a new method of coloring brain preparations, said to him amiably: "Your methods will make you famous yet," as though he had read Freud's most secret thoughts. Von Fleischl-Marxow became Freud's friend, and everyone in the master's entourage showed him a kindness he would not have dared to hope for; these men cured him of his sense of inferiority. He wrote to Martha: "The same men whom I have admired from afar as inaccessible, I now meet on equal terms and they show me their friendship."[28] It was the same with Charcot, who both at the Salpetrière hospital and in his home gave Freud a warm welcome very different from what

Viennese officialdom had long led him to expect; he was not only filled with admiration for the great physician but also deeply grateful to the kindly man who succeeded in giving him self-confidence at a time when he was suffering keenly from his poverty and unworldliness and weighed down with doubts as to his chances of success.[29]

Obviously Freud did not think exclusively of getting ahead, for if he had, his prospects at the age of forty for the future would undoubtedly have been brighter and more in keeping with his talents. If the two benefits that he expected of science—a great discovery that would make him famous and admittance to "good," enlightened society—are so heavily stressed in his dreams, it is solely because they were among his thwarted ambitions. In those years at the turn of the century that would decide his fate, Freud was suffering from a painful inner conflict. The two sides to which he belonged very unequally—the one part and parcel of his immediate experience, the other merely desired—now pressed him to choose between them once and for all; he had to decide whether to remain what he was, "a wretched old Jew," as he described himself to Fliess, or forcibly to wrest the first place he coveted from a hostile world, or to resign himself to some sort of compromise. But in his situation no choice was possible, nor would any compromise have been truly viable, for on the one hand he was a Jew, a fact implying a whole body of sentiments, desires, habits and ideas, that no effort of the will could efface; while on the other hand, he was an Austrian or German intellectual, and as such dominated by desires and needs which, though quite natural in his adoptive environment, were only partly in keeping with his nature. Hence the two sets of aspirations, sometimes parallel, sometimes divergent, and sometimes distinctly incompatible. His dreams were divided between them. And hence above all the two groups of characters in his dream play, embodying the conflict between his old loyalties and his new ambitions.

We are now in a position to understand the two columns of the table in which the dreamer of the *Traumdeutung* noted the main elements of his inner existence during the long gestation of the work. On the Jewish side, he was sincerely attached to his origins and firmly resolved not to betray them; though without religious beliefs of any kind, he remained faithful to the memory of his remote ancestors, showed extraordinary piety toward his father, and built his own home around an essential core of Jewish life. Here, on the Jewish side, he lived in direct communication with the people to whose Story and stories he was so devoted; here his culture was not a matter of learning; it was popular, vibrant with sympathy for the sufferings, the vitality, and the inimitable spirit of the humblest Jews. On the other side, he was devoured by ambition, and for that very reason open to all manner of temptations. Extraordinarily confident in his future glory through all the ups and downs of his career, yet at the same time tormented by self-doubt, he seized upon the most effective weapon at his disposal, namely, the humanist thought at the base of European culture and underlying the very idea of science. Though his desire to rise in the world did not make him into a bourgeois, it did cut him off entirely from "the people," whom he feared without knowing them because he regarded them as an unpredictable mass, ready to run wild at any moment. In his acute need of acceptance and recognition, he allowed himself to be dazzled for a short while by the Paris salons, but only for a short while, because his strict morality and innate sense of truth prevented him from doing what he would have had to do to gain access to them.

Thus, as he describes himself in the *Traumdeutung*, Freud always had two different roles to play, and sometimes they were contradictory. On the one hand, he was the son of Jakob Freud, the faithful pupil of Samuel Hammerschlag, the friend and collaborator of Josef Breuer, the Jewish doctor who delivered lectures to the B'nai B'rith, the simple man who all his life retained his attachment to his childhood friends and who shared their austere life, their traditional pleasures, and their cares. On the other hand, he was the spiritual son of foreign "fathers": Brücke, Helmholtz,

Meynert, and Charcot; in culture he was the son of Goethe,[30] Schiller, Virgil, Sophocles, Shakespeare, and in the end—it was indeed an end or a memorable beginning— he discovered a secret kinship with the ill-fated son of old king Laius, which elevated him not only to the glory he had so coveted, but even to a kind of royalty. Between these two sets of desires and roles which never fully coincided in the dreamer's conscious life, the coded imagery of the *Traum-deutung* established strong and incontestable ties. And thereby it revealed to Freud the true cause of his procrastination, for by associating the real figures of his everyday surroundings—his father, uncles, sons, and Jewish friends— with the mythical heroes of his unavowed ambitions, he at last gained an insight into what had always deterred him at the last moment from taking decisive action, namely, the hostility of his Jewish environment to the prestigious "others," who were calling him to join their ranks.

IV

YOU ARE REQUESTED TO CLOSE THE EYES*

* In German and in French "Close your eyes" and "Close the eyes," i.e., someone else's eyes, are the same. Tr.

Lovers of high-flown fantasies far removed from the petty concerns of everyday life are bound to be disappointed by Freud's dreams as recorded in the *Traumdeutung*. They are full of amusing inventions and poetic absurdities characteristic of dreams, but they do not transport us into a strange, enchanted world transcending our experience. These dreams are down-to-earth, barely irrational enough to be recognizable as dreams, often brief, full of jokes and ingenious neologisms. What makes them seem beautiful is chiefly Freud's extraordinary method of interpretation. Starting from absurd or trifling details, he pieces together the meaning of the whole by simple chains of reasoning, dazzling with logic and truth. In themselves they are pedestrian, and we know why: because Freud put his most obsessive preoccupations into them, his isolation as a scientist, his uncertainty about his therapeutic method, his rivalry with better-equipped colleagues, his crushing debts and perpetual need of money. He did not dream them for the pleasure of escaping, but in order to orient his thoughts, to achieve self-understanding through these complicated puzzles whose secret key no one had ever discovered, to gain control over everything that was amiss beneath his unruffled surface. He did not dream for the sake of dreaming, but in order to know himself as deeply and surely as mortal man with his limited consciousness can ever know himself. In this sense, he might justifiably have given the *Traumdeutung* the title, *Fantasies of a Realist,* which in that same year, 1899, a Viennese philosopher and scientist gave to his own dream book.[1]

The first of these "fantasies" to be analyzed[2] introduces persons whom the dreamer himself described as friends or relatives and who as such reappear in most of the major examples recorded in the *Traumdeutung*—anonymously, but with features so marked that one can hardly doubt their identity. First there is Irma, the heroine of the dream drama, whom Freud represents both as a patient and as a friend. (According to Jones she was his "favorite patient" at the time.) Irma was a young widow whom Freud thought hysterical and despite their friendship undertook to treat. After a time, he broke off the treatment because the patient persisted in not getting better, or, as the dream record puts it, in rejecting his "solution." What made this rejection especially mortifying was precisely that Irma was one of his few close friends. Indeed there is every reason to believe that, as one highly perceptive author[3] suggests, the young widow of the dream was none other than Anna Hammerschlag, the daughter of the old Hebrew teacher to whom Freud went for help in times of discouragement and whom he regarded as a kind of spiritual godfather to his children. (He named his second daughter Sophie after Sophie Schwab, Samuel Hammerschlag's niece, and he would give the name Anna to his last daughter, who was then about to be born.) As though to corroborate this theory, Irma is surrounded in the dream by three men who were also good friends of the family: Otto, i.e., Oskar Rie, the family physician and pediatrician; Leopold, i.e., Ludwig Rosenstein, also a pediatrician and related to Rie; and Dr. M., i.e., Josef Breuer, with whom Freud had collaborated for years; they had broken since the publication of the joint work because of a basic disagreement about the etiology of hysteria. The patient and the three doctors are the guests of Martha Freud (who was on friendly terms with all the protagonists of the dream). Martha seems to be suffering from a strange ailment. (Faithful to his resolution not to speak of sex, Freud tells us nothing of her condition, but we learn of it from a letter to Fliess: she was simply expecting her sixth child.)[4] And in the background we perceive still other figures who, though less clearly delineated, are equally important for the dreamer's inner life and the over-all meaning of the dream: Ernst von Fleischl-Marxow, whom Freud loved as "one of Creation's precious achievements," and whose end he was painfully aware of having hastened[5]; a former patient named Mathilda (like Freud's eldest daughter), whose death he had caused with injections of sulphonal, either because he administered them improperly or because he was ignorant of possible counterindications; and, of course, Wilhelm Fliess, who was very much alive but unfortunately detained in remote Berlin at a time when Freud needed his advice and encouragement more than ever. The dream reconstitutes the restricted sphere of Freud's affections and activities: the Breuers and the Hammerschlags lived in the same apartment house; Sophie Schwab had been engaged to Josef Paneth, one of the ghosts that haunt the *Traumdeutung*, a close friend of Freud's, who had died young of tuberculosis; Martha was close to Irma-Anna Hammerschlag, who had as a friend another frustrated young widow, probably the wife of the Nathan Weiss who had recently hanged himself on his return from his honeymoon[6]; Fliess had married Ida Bondy, a Viennese woman who had been Breuer's patient; Oskar Rie, Ludwig Rosenstein, and Freud played cards every week at the house of Königstein the ophthalmologist, who occurs frequently in the *Traumdeutung* in connection with the complicated cocaine affair. (Königstein had discovered the used of cocaine in surgery almost at the same time as Koller.)[7] With the exception of Fleischl, all the characters in the dream were members of the same close-knit group, inhabiting the same moral and sentimental universe; all were connected by marriage, friendship, and professional ambition, and sometimes there were still other ties between them. (Freud owed money to Königstein and Breuer; he had previously borrowed from Hammerschlag, Fleischl, and Paneth. The death of the last two prevented him from paying his debts, and this is the reality which accounts for the debt and guilt motifs in subsequent dreams.) If to this small number of background characters we add Amalia and Jakob Freud, who would of course soon occupy the center of the stage, and an assortment of brothers, uncles, and children who would appear in other dreams, we shall have more or less exhausted the group of Freud's familiars. It was a group with a very special character, offering remarkably little variety, yet apparently this group was capable of revealing something hitherto unknown about human relations, for it was there and nowhere else that psychoanalysis with all its potential universality was born.

The Irma dream develops two central themes that recur with greater or lesser variations in later dreams: on the one hand guilt, on the other an elaborate demonstration of innocence. Freud feels guilty because he has not cured Irma despite the hopes he aroused in her. This failure provides Oskar Rie and especially Breuer, the Dr. M. of the dream, whom he calls in as consultants, with an irrefutable argument against his theories. But in reality he is not to blame; it is Irma's fault if she has not recovered, for she has rejected the one "solution"[8] that would have made successful treatment possible. Her continued illness is also the fault of Otto, who was clumsy in giving her an injection, and may even have used a dirty needle. To top it all, she probably has organic troubles, which would clear Freud of all responsibility, since physical ailments cannot be the concern of a psychotherapist. As for Dr. M., he says such stupid things that he comes out of the dream entirely discredited, which is no doubt one of the main purposes of the dream. Thus Freud wins his case against himself: he is not the charlatan his friends and even his own family take him for (Martha refuses to let him examine her, thus siding with the recalcitrant patients who reject his "solution"). If people had faith in his method, he would cure them. It's all the fault of others: others prevent him from being a good doctor; others kill their patients with toxic substances and unclean syringes; others are stupid, stubborn, and narrow-minded. Thanks to this adroit shifting of wrongs—a mechanism that would later be termed "projection"—a mechanism that would later be termed "projection"—Freud is able to whitewash himself and take revenge at the same time, and his next step is to convince himself that his contested method is good in spite of appearances and that even if he is alone against the whole world he is right in persevering. Finally, the Irma dream, once decoded, corresponds perfectly to the real facts of his life, so confirming the soundness of the psychoanalytic method and justifying its generalized use.

In this first sample of decoding, which precedes the others by more than a year, Freud always shows a tendency to conceal his inferences wholly or in part, as soon as they come too close to his private life. Concerning his relations with Martha he gives us only the barest hints (rather unkind ones to be sure), and he tells us even less about the affection mingled with exasperation that he seems to have felt for Irma. In the latent content of the dream, sexuality is almost entirely divested of its erotic function; sexual desire is replaced by the desire to be right, and amorous passion becomes the ambitious pursuit of an idea. Purified by censorship of its specific emotions and jealousies, sex, which is after all the main motif of the dream—for what otherwise would be the point in this story of a pregnant woman and of frustrated young widows—resolves itself into a purely scientific question, the crux of which is no longer an affair of the heart, but wounded vanity and self-esteem.

If Freud expected to avoid embarrassment by suppressing the sexual content of his dreams, he must soon have realized that he was far from obtaining the desired result, for what his analysis thus brought to the surface was just as unpleasant to divulge as the intimacies he wished to keep secret. To compromise a patient and at the same time betray the confidence of a friend; to represent his old friend Oskar Rie as an incompetent doctor; to disparage Breuer, who enjoyed great authority in Freud's circle, by making him talk like a complete idiot ("It's an infection, think nothing of it," he says of Irma's illness) was to reveal a baseness, a "villainy," sufficient to discredit him in the eyes of the people he loved and respected, especially since none of these people had yet experienced the modern variant of the descent into the underworld, that is, the descent into the savagery and chaos of the unconscious. To make matters worse, the persons compromised by the dream were precisely those among whom Freud had to go on living; if they recognized themselves in the caricatures turned up by his analysis and resented his "revelations," his life would soon become unbearable. Hence his perplexity and the need to break off his associations, not only when they approached the forbidden sexual subjects, but also when they drove him to the seemingly more inoffensive theme of his ambition and the little "villainies" in which it involved him.[9]

This unforeseen difficulty may explain why he hesitated so long before interpreting another dream, for otherwise, now that he was in possession of a duly tested method, one might have expected him to waste no time in applying it. Be that as it may, it was almost a year before he analyzed, or at least before he published his analysis of, another dream, which we shall call the "You are requested to close the eyes" dream. It dated from November 23, 1896; Freud had dreamed it in the night after his father's funeral and he communicated it to Fliess some days later, with a very sketchy analysis (the analysis is even sketchier in the *Traumdeutung*, where the importance of the dream's content is minimized and the dream serves merely to illustrate one of those absurd ambiguities in which the unconscious seems to take pleasure. After referring to the dream as "pretty," Freud goes on to write: "I found myself in a shop where there was a notice up saying:

> You are requested
> to close the eyes.

"I recognized the place as the barber's to which I go every day. On the day of the funeral I was kept waiting, and therefore arrived at the house of mourning rather late. The family were displeased with me, because I had arranged for the funeral to be quiet and simple, which they later agreed was the best thing. They also took my lateness in rather bad part. The phrase on the notice-board has a double meaning. It means 'one should do one's duty towards the dead' in two senses—an apology, as though I had not done my duty

and my conduct needed overlooking, and the actual duty itself. The dream was thus an outlet for the feeling of self-
reproach which a death generally leaves among the survivors."[10] The editor of the letters to Fliess saw fit to note
that Freud relates the same dream in the *Traumdeutung*, but
"in greater detail, obviously with the aid of notes."[11] Actually the *Traumdeutung* version is not more detailed than that
of the letter, nor does it seem more faithful; on the contrary,
it appears to have been arbitrarily reworked. There is no
mention of waiting at the barber's, nor of arriving late at the
house of mourning, nor of any sense of guilt; the sign no
longer suggests a barber shop but the "No Smoking" signs
seen in trains; the text itself is more impersonal,[12] and now
offers an alternate: *"You are requested to close the eyes/or
an eye,"*[13] which gives the phrase a new ambiguity. Only the
disagreement between Freud and his family about the ceremony is common to the two versions, but in the *Traumdeutung* it is very much toned down and concerns only
"some other members of the family,"[14] who moreover were
in the wrong because in choosing the simpler ceremony
Freud had done just what his father would have wished. In
both cases certain aspects of the funeral are left in the dark.
Did the family really find fault with Freud for its simplicity? Or were they shocked because he wished to do away
with the religious ceremony or reduce it to a minimum?
In view of Freud's lateness, the latter would seem the
more likely explanation of the dream conflict, for Sigmund
and the family probably disagreed about Jakob Freud's religious beliefs. If this is the case, it becomes clear why Freud,
in the dream, starts by accusing himself of impiety and then
proceeds to exculpate himself. In any case the published version tells us not more but much less than the text sent to
Fliess,[15] which itself provides a very much watered-down
analysis. Both provisionally sidestep the problem of guilt, the
first by dating the dream on the day before the funeral, so
eliminating Freud's real offense, i.e., arriving late for the funeral; the second by speaking of a "feeling of self-reproach
which a death generally leaves among the survivors,"[16] so

glossing over his own guilt. His "descent into the underworld" had not yet begun (it was not undertaken until several months later, during the summer of 1897) and the Oedipus complex toward which he had long been groping had not yet been described or given its fateful name.

In disposing of the keen sense of guilt aroused in him by his father's death as the "feeling of self-reproach which a death generally leaves among the survivors"—so avoiding the disagreeable discoveries to which a deeper analysis would have led him—Freud was able to distract his attention for the time being from the cluster of violent and conflicting desires that he would be obliged to confront later on. In other words, he obeyed the command to "close the eyes," employed by the dream in the intention of absolving and at the same time accusing him. (The accusation derives from the very same elements with the help of which the dream tries to exculpate him.) But a few months later he had another dream, a very obscure one, whose very absurdity obligated him to look into his case more closely, that is, to take one step more toward his long-postponed self-analysis. This was the "uncle with the yellow beard" dream, which he develops at length in the *Traumdeutung*, while at the same time giving the reader to understand that he had deliberately abridged his interpretation. Once again the real events elaborated and transposed in the dream are closely connected with Freud's hopes of a professorship, which had received some encouragement in January 1897, when, as we have seen, Nothnagel informed Freud that Krafft-Ebing, Frankl-Hochwart, and himself had suggested his name to the Faculty Council, reserving the right to appeal directly to the minister if the Faculty Council were not disposed to accept their recommendation. For fear of raising undue hopes, Nothnagel had spoken in his letter of "other" obstacles to Freud's appointment, and Freud wrote to Fliess that he had no illusions. Thereupon he met N., a Jewish friend, who congratulated him on being finally about to obtain satisfaction—a possibility denied to him, N., once and for all, not exactly because he was a Jew, but because he had once been accused of a crime and this was held against him even though the accusation had been dropped as unfounded. Since there was nothing of that kind in Freud's past, said N., he had good reason to hope. But R., another friend, whom certain indications enable us to identify as Dr. Königstein, presented the situation in a much less favorable light. A longtime candidate, weary of being "forgotten" over and over again, R. had decided to get to the bottom of the matter and gone to the ministry, where he asked whether his Jewish origin was the main barrier to his promotion. There he was given to understand that this was indeed the case, and that same evening he told Freud about it. The following night Freud had a dream which he broke down into two parts: "1) . . . My friend R. was my uncle.—I had a great feeling of affection for him. 2) I saw before me his face, somewhat changed. It was as though it had been drawn out lengthwise. A yellow beard that surrounded it stood out especially clearly."[17] The manifest absurdity of the dream seems to dispense the dreamer with the need to take it seriously; obviously it had no meaning, and it would be a waste of time to try to find one. But Freud soon realized that he was reasoning just as his patients did when analysis of their dreams threatened to touch a sore spot. Alerted, moreover, by the extraordinary repugnance inspired by this stupid dream, he decided to lay bare the causes of his strange "resistance" by honestly applying his method to himself. He starts with the uncle theme: " 'R. was my uncle.' What could that mean? I never had more than one uncle—Uncle Josef. There was an unhappy story attached to him. Once—more than thirty years ago—in his eagerness to make money, he allowed himself to become involved in a transaction of a kind that is severely punished by the law, and he was in fact punished for it. My father, whose hair turned grey from grief in a few days, used always to say that Uncle Josef was not a bad man but only a simpleton; those were his words."[18]

So Uncle Josef had been imprisoned for theft. But why

does Freud speak of him as his only uncle? Actually, as he explains in a note appended to the above passage, he had known five of his uncles, and especially one whom he greatly loved and admired: "But at the moment at which I overcame my resistance to interpreting the dream I said to myself that I never had more than one uncle—the one intended in the dream."[19] Who was this favorite uncle, whom Freud says he admired but whom he does not name here? Josef, one is inclined to think, since this is the only name that comes to his mind and since he mentions no other in any of his work.[20] Be that as it may, he remains vague on this point, purposely no doubt, not only because Uncle Josef was not a very commendable character—from the standpoint of society he was a common criminal, and his own brother called him a simpleton—but also because Freud's family was not without its taints. This we know from a letter written ten years earlier to Martha, bidding her think twice before agreeing to marry him: "I have never told you about my uncle in Breslau, because I never think of him. I have seen him three times in my life, on each occasion for a quarter of an hour. He is a younger brother of my father, a rather ordinary man, a merchant, and the story of his family is very sad. Of the four children only one daughter is normal; she is married in Poland. One son is a hydrocephalic and feeble-minded; another, who as a young man showed some promise, went insane at the age of nineteen, and a daughter went the same way when she was twenty-odd. I had so completely forgotten this uncle that I have always thought of my own family as free from any hereditary taint. But since I have been thinking about Breslau[21] it all comes back to me, and I am afraid the fact that one of the sons of my other (very unfortunate) uncle in Vienna died an epileptic is something I cannot shift to his mother's side, with the result that I have to acknowledge to a considerable 'neuropathological taint,' as it is called."[22] In view of the enormous importance he then attached to hereditary factors in the etiology of psychic and neurological disorders, he was bound to blame this hereditary taint for the "nicely developed tendency toward neurasthenia" from which he had been suffering for some time and which was also present in his sister Rosa and his brother Emmanuel. "As a neurologist," he wrote, "I am about as worried by such things as a sailor is by the sea." His concluding remark—"These things are very common in Jewish families"[23]—makes his revelations somewhat less damaging to the Freud family but brings out his opinion that anyone with the deteriorated blood of the Jewish race in his veins could expect to inherit and transmit such taints. Thus it is not at all surprising that in interpreting his dream Freud should have "forgotten" the existence of his wayward or mentally deficient uncles; they reminded him too much of the congenital taints, a share in which he was afraid of having inherited, if only in the attenuated form of a "nicely developed tendency toward neurasthenia."

Thus when his dream led him to think of an uncle, Freud forgot this whole paternal branch, all of whom were more or less degenerate; but he could hardly fail to mention Josef, who lived in Vienna and must have been on intimate terms with the family, since Jakob Freud had felt great affection for his unfortunate brother. But this Josef had an epileptic son, and Jakob Freud had regarded Josef himself as a "simpleton"; in any event his mere name sufficed to remind Freud of his burden of Jewishness, which he had thought he could forget by disavowing his tainted uncles and cousins. Josef's role in the "uncle with the yellow beard" dream was, indeed, to show the dreamer that unconsciously he was very unhappy about his origins, and was prepared to do anything, even to betray his brothers and friends, in order to deliver himself of this heavy burden.

It was in order to avoid this knowledge that Freud at first declared this dream to be absurd, much too absurd to warrant analysis. For once Uncle Josef was drawn into the chain of Freud's associations, everything fitted in so neatly and formed so close a mesh that he could no longer "close his eyes" to his ugly thoughts. His friend R., who was his uncle, or more precisely his uncle Josef (since while interpreting the dream he imagined that he had no other uncle) was connected of course with the affair of the professorship, which Freud had discussed the previous evening with Dr. König-stein, who had taken a dim view of it. Uncle Josef, as we know, was both criminal and feeble-minded; thus he represented a combination of N., who was barred from promotion because a false denunciation had got him into difficulties with the law, and of R. who, having committed no crime, could stand only for the other racial and family taint, to wit, feeble-mindedness. Thus the dream explained everything to the dreamer's best advantage: what stood in the way of Freud's two colleagues' advancement was not that they were Jewish, but their unworthiness, the one because of a questionable police record, the other because of his imbecility. So since Freud was neither an imbecile nor a suspected criminal, he could anticipate the ministry's decision with confidence.

Deeply disturbed to find that he *unconsciously* nourished such revolting feelings toward men for whom in his waking state he felt only affection and respect, astonished and dismayed to learn that he *unconsciously* wished to dissociate himself from his fellow Jews so as to escape their humiliating lot, Freud, who still did not admit and would never readily admit the full extent of his ambitions, searched his memory for an explanation of his dreams, so far removed from what he believed to be his true character and outlook. He soon remembered the two prophecies that had been made him at different moments in his childhood, the one, rather vague, that he would be a great man, the other, more precise, that he was destined to become a cabinet minister. Especially the second prophecy, as we have seen, made a profound and apparently indelible impression on him. (More than thirty years had elapsed between the prophecy and its realization in a dream.) This prophecy dated from the days of the "middle class ministry" and the famous quip about every industrious Jewish schoolboy carrying "a Cabinet minister's portfolio in his school satchel." Now we begin to understand the function of the dream. Freud devised it first in order to bring back a happy past and second to console himself, get revenge, and establish himself "on the other side," with a new identity: "It began to dawn on me that my dream had carried me back from the dreary present to the cheerful hopes of the days of the *'Bürger'* Ministry, and that the wish that it had done its best to fulfil was one dating back to those times. In abusing my two learned and eminent colleagues because they were Jews, and in treating the one as a simpleton and the other as a criminal, I was behaving as though I were the Minister, I had put myself in the Minister's place. Turning the tables on His Excellency with a vengeance! He had refused to appoint me *professor extraordinarius*, and I had retaliated in the dream by stepping into his shoes."[24] Thus in abusing his two Jewish friends, Freud was not only trying to reassure himself about his prospects of promotion; more important, he wanted to break once and for all with his Jewishness, with all its inner perils —hereditary diseases—and outward disadvantages for an ambitious man determined to rise in the world. That is why he changed places with Count von Härtel, not only ceasing to be persecuted and becoming a persecutor, but also, in his new capacity of minister and nobleman, rising to the summit of sordid calculation, courageous in the defense of his ideas; he belonged in real life.

Today it is hard to realize how keenly Freud suffered because of this struggle to which his self-analysis drove him, a struggle for which he was no better equipped than other men of his generation. (After all, he was alone, without the decisive help a patient receives from his analyst.) He knew that in his conscious life he was moral, generous, incapable of sordid calculation, courageous in the defense of his ideas; he knew that he was still a loyal Jew, even though he had lost the traditional faith. But now he discovered within himself a baseness, a pettiness, a malice worthy of a genuine "villain"; and to make matters worse, by an irony inherent in his method, his only hope of recovering from this collapse of moral values lay in delving still deeper and shattering still more of his illusions. Now we understand why he was at first so reluctant and why later, when better informed, he kept to himself a good part of what he dredged up from the depths of his unconscious. Not that he really concealed the central and most disturbing element (his unconscious desire to disavow the Jewish father whom he held responsible for his taints, his poverty, and his social humiliation); but he revealed it only indirectly, in fragmented allusions and images, which he sometimes left almost transparent and sometimes deliberately blurred, as though he had wished to offer the attentive reader the key to his "family novel," while at the same time doing everything in his power to keep it away from him.[25]

When we piece together the fragments of self-knowledge which Freud scattered throughout his work for purposes of demonstration, but never combined into a meaningful whole, it becomes clear that in its own way the autobiographical part of the *Traumdeutung* represents Freud's "family novel" —a discontinuous but coherent novel in which the themes of disavowal and imaginary filiation take on relatively discreet forms consonant with the dreamer's real age.[26] This piecing together is not always possible on the basis of an isolated dream; more often than not it is necessary to compare all the dreams relating to the same preoccupations, to date them, study their shadings, and in some instances consult other documents, such as letters, which, because they are more direct, can help to rectify a certain intentional vagueness, or to fill gaps resulting from repression. In his analysis of the "uncle with the yellow beard" dream Freud omits all reference to heredity. But if we wish to know why, whether the omission was deliberate or whether he had thrust back everything connected with this troublesome subject into the darkness of the unconscious, we must look to outside evidence. The letter to Martha shows us that the chain of associations uncle-criminal-idiot had occurred to him at least once, leading him to make the pessimistic statements about his own mental health and the drawbacks of a Jewish heredity. And such statements were just what was needed to justify the disavowal that Freud was trying to accomplish in his dreams and daydreams: if Jewish fathers are guilty of begetting mentally deficient and morally tainted children, then Jewish sons can be forgiven for inventing genealogies from which their real fathers and real ancestors are excluded.

Of course this "novel" with its disjointed episodes lacks the naïveté of the infantile fable from which it ultimately derives. Obviously Freud did not regard himself as the son of a king or as the illegitimate descendant of some nobleman; apparently, he did not even remember early fantasies of this kind, or he would surely have related them to the two prophecies of his early childhood, which had made so strong an impression on him. He confined himself to representing, and satisfying, in dreams the desire to be someone else, the child of a different father in a different time and place—and analysis forced him to acknowledge that this was the motive behind his phantasms. This desire for total transformation is evident throughout, even in the secondary developments where the family myth is not in evidence. As one might expect, however, it follows the development of the inner crisis recorded in the *Traumdeutung;* first masked or expressed in an attenuated form, it gains force and freedom as the dreamer approaches the truth.

Thus in the first dream of the book—the Irma dream—this desire to be someone else is almost entirely eclipsed by the desire to be right, which is its main justification. Believing that his Jewish friends think him ignorant and professionally incompetent, Freud accuses Oskar Rie, Rosenstein, and Breuer of the same failings. Even here, however, the main purpose of this apparent defense is obviously to discredit Breuer who, because he is older than the dreamer and regarded as an authority in his social group, embodies paternal authority, but a feeble, ridiculous authority, based on stupidity and incompetence. While examining Irma, Breuer makes idiotic remarks; consequently he is an idiot, as Uncle Josef would later be, and through him of course Jakob Freud, against whom in reality the whole scenario is directed. Breuer is the first link in the chain of arguments that Freud was unconsciously to forge against his father, in order to provide himself with a reason for disavowing him.

There seems to be much less hostility in the "close the eyes" dream, though the father figure is directly under attack; instead of attacking others, the dreamer merely pleads for indulgence, as though there were nothing very serious about Sigmund's wrongs toward Jakob and they were entirely a product of the circumstances (the funeral). In the "uncle" dream the guilt theme is again discernible through the composite figure of friend R. (uncle and friend being telescoped because of their yellow beards). But here all the blame is shifted to Jakob who, by begetting Sigmund, has put him in a position of inferiority for life.[27] To punish him for being his father, the son gets rid of him by taking the name and function of Count von Härtel, a move that satisfies all his desires because through it he casts off his troublesome origins and sets himself up in a leading position "on the other side."

That this is the aim toward which he has been tending all along is demonstrated by another dream, probably dating from the same period, that is cited not in the *Traumdeutung*, but in a short book that Freud wrote somewhat later[28] as a guide to his intricate theory of dreams. Remarkable for the contrast between its conciseness and the richness of its latent content, this dream has become a classical example of "condensation." Freud sees himself sitting in a railway compartment. On his knees he is holding a rather peculiar top hat: it is made of transparent glass. At first this object makes him think of the proverb: "*Mit dem Hute in der Hand kommt man durch has ganze Land*" ("With hat in hand, you can cross the entire land"). Next "the glass cylinder [German *Zylinder*=top hat] led me to think of an incandescent gas mantle; and I soon saw that I should like to make a discovery which would make me as rich and independent as my fellow-countryman Dr. Auer von Welsbach was made by his."[29] Since the celebrated chemist was a baron, Freud thus disavowed his origins and ennobled himself by the sheer force of desire, without conflict and apparently without guilt.

The situation is very different in a later dream (June 1898) cited in the *Traumdeutung*. Here Freud, now in a much more advanced stage of his self-analysis, is still obsessed by the problem of his position in the world, but, it would seem, vaguely tempted by a new solution. His envy of aristocratic titles, symbols of the privileged birth which figured so prominently in his "family novel," is replaced by a radically opposite attitude, one of open revolt against the nobility in general and against the intolerably smug and mediocre aristocrats in positions of power. Here Freud is no longer a double of Count von Härtel or Baron Auer von Welsbach, but the resolute adversary of Count von Thun, then Austrian Prime Minister (or of Count Taaffe, his predecessor; the dream is vague on this point). On the day preceding this dream, which he himself terms "revolutionary," Freud had been engaged in a daydream revolving around the same grievances. He had gone to the West Station to take the train to Bad Aussee, where his family was spending the summer holiday. An early train, going to Ischl, was still standing in the station, and to his extreme indignation Freud had seen Count Thun, who was on his way to Ischl for an audience with the Emperor, board it without showing a ticket.[30] Fuming about the arrogance and unjustified privileges of the nobility, he began to hum a tune which he himself recognized as Figaro's aria from *Le Nozze di Figaro*, "*Se vuol ballare, signor contino . . .*" That helped to sustain his belligerent mood: "And now all kinds of insolent and revolutionary ideas were going through my head, in keeping with Figaro's words and with my recollections of Beaumarchais' comedy which I had seen acted by the *Comédie française*. I thought of the phrase about the great gentlemen who had taken the trouble to be born . . . and of how our malicious opposition journalists made jokes over Count Thun's name, calling him instead 'Count Nichtsthun' (Count Do-Nothing). Not that I envied him. He was on his way to a difficult audience with the Emperor, while I was

the real Count Do-Nothing—just off on my holidays."[81]
Thus in his daydream Freud had once again ennobled himself by ironically giving himself an absurd title: but then another privileged gentleman deprived him of the only available seat in the train, so that to his boundless indignation he
was obliged to spend the night in a coach without a corri-
dor, and consequently without access to any toilet. "I complained to an official, without any success; but I got my own
back on him by suggesting that he should make a hole in the
floor of the compartment to meet the possible needs of pas-
sengers." Here again a train is a scene of persecution and un-
pleasantness for Freud; again he is made to feel inferior
(such incidents probably accounted for his dread of trains),
but now he no longer contents himself as he did ten years
before with replying angrily to the insults of a few dolts;
this time he is seized with such hatred for the whole of society that he regards himself as a revolutionary—though only
in a dream and, in accordance with the whimsical logic of
the unconscious, motivated at least as much by an urgent
need—a need which society prevents him from satisfying in
the train—as by a sudden flare-up of revolutionary passion.

In his dream, Freud opposes Count von Thun in a meeting of students and is surprised at his own behavior. The
interpretation, conducted with brio and even a sort of
playfulness, reveals a wide range of interlocking motifs from
Mozart's *Figaro* to the student Adolf Fischhof and memories
of the 1848 revolution. Here again of course megalomania is
the dominant theme—Count Nichtsthun is the equal of
Count Thun of the daydream—but now Freud develops it
for the benefit of the opposite camp; in attacking the Prime
Minister, Freud is emulating the great Jewish revolutionary
leaders who fought and are still fighting for freedom (he
associates Adolf Fischhof, the revolutionary hero of the
past, with Victor Adler, the Socialist leader of his own day,
with whom he had gone to secondary school). Thus the dilemma in which he has been struggling in vain—to be a good
Jew and retreat into himself, or to go over triumphantly to
the other side—is by no means a fatality, but appears to be

only if one lacks the courage to break through it; actually there is a third possibility which consists, as the Heines and Börnes knew, in declaring war on society as a whole. The dream, however, does not end with this daring proposition; the last scene brings Freud back to the threshold of his daily life in the company of an elderly invalid. Probably in the role of a nurse, Freud hands him a urinal (symbol at once of the most prosaic aspect of his profession, of the need which will soon awaken him, and of the ideas of grandeur which set the dream in motion).[32] The entrance of this ailing old gentleman, whom Freud cares for with a devotion that is rather humiliating in view of the particular service he renders, obliges him to leave the heroic sphere and descend abruptly to earth: he is no longer a rebellious son, but rather the loving son of Jakob Freud; and he is no longer the revolutionary destined to play the heroic role of a savior, but the modest physician whose mission it is at best to relieve people's sufferings.

Just as Freud's conflict with Count Thun conceals the secret desire to disavow his origins—Count Do-Nothing is not serious; and moreover, if Freud rebels against the mighty of this world, against powerful men and fathers in general, it is precisely in order to remain faithful to his own father, since in embracing the revolutionary cause he identifies with Jewish heroes—so his relations, real as well as dreamed, with the city of Rome lay bare the complex motives that impelled him to rewrite his life in the noble or sublime manner, and thus to break through the limitations of his identity. Rome, as we know, symbolized in his eyes what was best and most precious in the "other side." For this reason it was an object of love and desire, something he coveted and to which he was irresistibly drawn, but to which he had no legitimate title. And because it seemed so far above him, so infinitely remote, he persuaded himself that if only he managed to get there he would succeed in all his undertakings, and in his private mythology Rome became associated with a kind of superstitious promise. The situation was further complicated, however, by the fact that "Rome" symbolizes two overlap-

ping but conflicting realities, which were as hostile to one
another in Freud's mind as they are in history, namely: Antiquity, which he had always admired, and the Church,
which he had always regarded as an enemy. But even
Roman Antiquity was not without its contradictions; on the
one hand it represented the lofty ideal of man that was a necessity to Freud; yet Freud was well aware that in the eyes
of the Jewish people "Rome" signified an odious political
power against which they once rebelled. Thus there was as
much to repel as to attract him in the thought of Rome: he
desired ardently to go there because he had come to believe
that this alone would guarantee and bear witness to his personal success (this magic tie would be acknowledged and
broken only after his first visit to Rome, and even then he
persisted in believing that he owed his new-found sense of
freedom to his visit to the Eternal City), but he always
recoiled at the last moment because his Jewish feeling opposed what it could not regard as a betrayal or at least as a
cowardly disavowal. In sum, there was only one way in
which he could enter Rome without disavowing his father
and his ancestors: as an armed conqueror, and this was pat-
ently impossible. That was why he had to content himself
for years with seeing Rome only in his dreams, until the moment when, having wrested its secret from the human unconscious, he was finally able to break the spell and walk the
streets of a city that had at last been reduced to earthly proportions as a plain tourist enamored of antiquity.

This extraordinary adventure, whose only protagonists are
a man and a city—a Jew and the mother-city of Christianity,
a modern man and the legend of his past—is known to us
through four dreams which Freud cites in the *Traumdeutung*, by way of demonstrating the insurmountable in-
fantilism of the psyche. The first of these "Roman" dreams
amounts to no more than a single image; looking out of the
window of a railway car, Freud discovers the Tiber and the
Ponte Sant' Angelo; the train has stopped, but it does not
even occur to him to get off. In the second, he sees the city
far in the distance; that at least is as much as he consents to

tell us, for by his own admission he has censored not only his analysis but also the manifest content of the dream: ". . . Another time someone led me to the top of a hill and showed me Rome half shrouded in mist; it was so far away that I was surprised at my view of it being so clear. There was more in the content of this dream than I feel prepared to detail; but the theme of 'the promised land seen from afar' was obvious in it."[33] In the third dream, Freud is at last in Rome, but is dismayed to find that "the scenery was not of urban character." Consequently he feels lost, and catching sight of a certain Herr Zucker whom he knows slightly, he asks his way. In the fourth dream his inhibition is indicated by the metamorphosis of Rome into a composite of Rome and Prague and the presence of posters written in German. Thus in each dream the city finds an ingenious way of evading the dreamer's vision, or rather the dreamer finds a way of concealing it from himself, and is thus enabled to cultivate his nostalgia without succumbing to the temptation it entails.

Since Freud's censorship consists here as usual in casting a veil over the delicate subjects of sexuality and maternal incest, his analysis of the Roman dreams is succinct and relatively superficial, and the desire for omnipotence seems to play a far more important role in it than desire or specifically "Oedipean" desire.[34] He does not even begin to analyze the first dream, but leaves the reader to unravel for himself the tangled threads leading to the Ponte Sant' Angelo and the castle of the same name; but this is none too difficult if we bear in mind that the Castel Sant' Angelo, at once a papal residence and an imperial Roman mausoleum, symbolizes defunct paganism as well as its very living Christian successor, and that Freud had only too many reasons to feel resentful toward both of them. The composite and for that very reason ambiguous Castle that he sees from the train brings him back just in time to his profoundly ambivalent feelings toward the city that has bewitched him; no, he will not leave the train, for in the mind of any Jew this fascinating city must stand both for abominable historical memories and for a present charged with new humiliations. Yet even this refusal to betray his people shows how strong the temptation is; he is so unsure of his power to resist it that to protect himself he forgoes his freedom of movement and literally paralyzes himself.

Freud's account of the second dream is truncated, and again the analysis is not carried very far; but its "manifest content" is in itself so revealing that it needs little interpretation and even throws light on the "blanks" that Freud has deliberately left in his account. The whole dream consists in a grandiose vision and a phrase—"The promised land seen from afar"—which the author hastens to qualify as a cliché, as though to conceal or attenuate its significance. Obviously both the vision and the phrase hark back to the Bible: Freud sees himself in the position of Moses when God makes him climb Mount Nebo and shows him in the distance the land of Canaan, on which because of his sin he can never set foot, but which, as he knows, the Jewish people is destined by divine decree to conquer and take root in. In the biblical context this revelation is both the Prophet's reward and his punishment: at last it is given him to see the Promised Land, but having done so he must die. Except in this one point—and here too perhaps, for the deep level of the unconscious which they sound, the two "Roman" dreams of the *Traumdeutung* are in some degree dreams of death—the concordance between the two situations is perfect: Freud is led to a hilltop, which implies that he does not go there of his own free will, but like Moses in obedience to some transcendent necessity; and there, despite the distance and the mist, the object of his nostalgia appears to him with incredible clarity, as though by magic. But no more than Moses will he know the joy of entering it; Rome remains inaccessible to him, as a punishment for some unknown sin. (One of the functions of the dream is precisely to cast a veil over the nature of this grave transgression.)

At first sight the mechanism seems simple enough: caught in the enchanted circle of thoughts and feelings inspired in him by the forbidden city, Freud boldly identifies himself with the most sublime figure in the Bible. This gives him an enormous narcissistic lift (for in the Jewish hierarchy no one surpasses Moses) and at the same time bolsters up the system of defense necessitated by his position. (He is always having to defend himself against an imaginary supreme judge, who is his father or himself, or more precisely, the father whose commandments have become a part of himself.) If Freud is one with Moses, then he can have nothing in common with the renegade Jew and disloyal son he is so much afraid of becoming when he ponders his ambitions; as the inspired leader, the spiritual man and political guide, the unique lawgiver of the Jewish people, he is obviously above all suspicion. And similarly, if Rome is identical with Canaan, it can no longer be regarded as the glamorous "other side" in which Freud aspires to settle, but is nothing more than the home of idolatrous, uncouth tribes, infected with superstition and for that reason doomed to extinction. For Freud-Moses the seduction of Rome-Canaan relates beyond the shadow of a doubt to what the Promised Land will become when the Law promulgated by him will have expelled idolatry from it forever, and not to what it is now with its false gods and abominations.[35] He could hardly have imagined a better way of exculpating himself: covered with the authority of Moses, he was irreproachable; now no one would dare to suspect him of wanting, even in vague daydreams, to deny or disavow his Jewishness.

The argument seems unanswerable, but on closer scrutiny it turns against its author, for Freud could not pretend to the warlike, political, and religious designs on Rome implied by his biblical comparison. First, he loved the city, and far from wanting to destroy the civilization it symbolized in his eyes, he yearned to see it, to admire the vestiges of its past grandeur at leisure and if possible appropriate them (by collecting ancient art objects). Unlike Moses, whose mission it was to obliterate the particularities of "the other side" and usher in the law of the desert, Freud wished to efface his own particularities and to resemble the Philistines of the foreign city. If he did not contemplate Rome-Canaan with the ideas of warlike prophet, he could look upon it only with those of the potential turncoat, whose thoughts of conquest, far from reflecting the contempt of a reformer, masked a total subservience to the alien culture. Thus in the last analysis the identification with Moses was a mere screen concealing the unavowable desires of a renegade and the insurmountable scruples that stood in the way of their fulfillment.[36]

Immediately after this evocation of the Promised Land comes the dream of the invisible Rome in which Freud, once again disappointed in his expectation, asks his way ("all roads lead to Rome") of a slight acquaintance, Herr Zucker. This last analysis, the most complete of the series and hence the richest in content, enables us to identify the two divergent directions that the dreamer tried, in apparent defiance of all good sense, to take both at once. The first chain of associations takes in Herr Zucker (sugar); diabetes (*Zuckerkrankheit*); Fliess, who was then engaged in research on diabetes, a so-called "constitutional disease"; Karlsbad, where Freud and Fliess usually sent their diabetic patients, and where they had arranged to meet the following Easter; Rome, which Freud had proposed to Fliess as the scene of this same meeting, but which Fliess had rejected; and finally the Jewish stowaway who hoped to reach Karlsbad, "if his constitution could stand it." The second chain of images and memories leads in the opposite direction, for here Karlsbad is replaced by ancient Rome and the unhappy Jewish stowaway by the warlike Hannibal, the Semitic hero in whom Freud as a child had admired the avenger of his people. Hannibal like Freud had been obliged to halt at Lake Trasimene and had been unable to capture the detested city. Thus in the first chain Freud, humiliated and beaten like the Jew traveling without a ticket, is prevented from going to Rome by a "constitutional disease," that is, by his Jewishness, for Jewishness as seen in the "Uncle Josef" dream is at once a taint and an obstacle to success, whereas in the second chain of associations, where Hannibal stands for "Jewish tenacity" in the face of Rome, symbol of "the Catholic church," Semitism is a mark of greatness. In reality, however, this opposition does not represent an alternative; what prevents Freud from going to Rome is his Jewishness, not a personal failing, but a hereditary and incurable disease. And even if his "constitution" could stand it, he would have to go to Rome on the sly, as a "stowaway," for he is neither able nor willing to pay for his admission ticket to Western civilization, which, as in Heine's day, is neither more nor less than baptism. But unfortunately Jewishness is not necessarily a drawback; witness Hannibal, who was too proud of his race and birth to humble himself (unlike the Jew on his way to Karlsbad, who humbled himself, *but did not give up*). And Hannibal also had the advantage of filial piety; his father Hamilcar had made him swear as a boy to take vengeance on the Romans, and his sole aim in all his campaigns was to fulfill his oath. True, his march on Rome was no more successful than Freud's, but the mere attempt encouraged the dreamer by proving that a great man can attack "the other side" without being seduced by the enemy.

Thus Freud was at once the ailing and impecunious Jew in the train to Karlsbad and the Carthaginian soldier in whose person the Semitic race reconquered its pride. Sickly, wretched, exposed to blows and sarcasm in one part of himself, in the other he was the epitome of Jewish courage and "tenacity" which no enemy had ever subdued. In Karlsbad he was sick, afflicted with the hereditary disease that prevented him from fulfilling his lofty destiny, but on the shores of Lake Trasimene he was strong, self-assured, full of courage and pride. In both cases, however, he could boast of absolute loyalty. The Jew on the train suffered so much only because he was a Jew in the eyes of all and refused to "pay the price of his ticket"; and Hannibal, too, kept faith with his birth and convictions, dying by his own hand rather than surrender to his triumphant enemies. This time the dreamer's system of defense seems to be really flawless: the little Jew, capable of adapting himself to anything, and the uncompromising Semite work hand in hand to prove the purity of Freud's intentions, even in the shadowy zone of his "Roman" desires, where they might seem grossly suspect.

But this comforting vision is not the end of the matter. A new ambiguity is introduced by a single sentence. This sentence—which points up a flaw in the system, is a quotation from Jean-Paul Richter. It was uttered by Freud in a waking state, while he was appraising his chances of passing through Rome on his way to Naples the following summer. The quotation is as follows: "Which of the two, it may be debated, walked up and down his study with the greater impatience after he had formed his plan of going to Rome—Winckelmann the Vice-Rector or Hannibal the Commander-in-Chief?" This new antithesis throws the whole system out of kilter. We know that Hannibal was utterly devoted to his work of vengeance, that no intellectual passion, no aesthetic fascination weakened his resolve. But what of Winckelmann? He was a famous eighteenth-century scholar, an archaeologist and art historian, who like Freud revered Rome as the true cradle of Western civilization.[87] Though a Protestant, Winckelmann, recognized by his contemporaries as a man of superior mind very much above the prejudices of the day, was offered the position of librarian to the pope, on condition that he "pay the price of his ticket," i.e., become converted to Catholicism. Driven by his irresistible passion for Rome and its antiquities, apparently indifferent to public opinion, he seems to have felt no great misgivings about embracing the Catholic religion. "It is the love of knowledge and nothing else," he wrote, "that leads me to consider the proposition that has been made me." Now Freud resembled Winckelmann in several ways. They both devoted the better part of themselves to science; both were poor and ambitious, an awkward combination that made them both solitary figures. And finally, they were both hostile to organized religion of all kinds.[88] Here we have more than enough to account for the at first sight incongruous quotation with which Freud was led in spite of himself to vary the formula of his vision.

Indeed, this variant not only adds a new touch of ambiguity to the dream, but inclines it in the very direction he did not wish to take. In the new cast of characters, Hannibal remains the intransigent Semite, condemned to failure precisely by his obstinate loyalty to his people and culture, but Winckelmann represents the emancipated man of science, the free thinker who rises above tribal considerations, who does not shrink back from apostasy for the sake of a purely intellectual passion and who through his apostasy achieves success. Here Freud is no longer confronted by a choice between two forms of fidelity, both leading to failure; now he is called upon to choose between a fidelity that fails and a betrayal crowned with success. And what was Freud's choice in the face of this explicit alternative? In defiance of all logic—though the logic of the unconscious is not that of reason—he chose Hannibal, with whom he had nothing in common but the fortuitous circumstance that neither was able to get to Rome, in opposition to Vice-Rector Winckelmann, who as a free thinker, a daring scientist, and a worshiper of the ancient world, was infinitely closer to his own intellectual sphere. If he preferred a soldier—something that he himself was not and never would be—to a man of science like himself, it was clearly because he attached the utmost importance to camouflaging his love of Rome as merciless hatred, thus abjuring the Winckelmann, the turncoat scientist, who lurked, or so he feared, within him. Hiding behind the Semitic soldier as he had previously hidden behind the Jewish prophet, Freud hoped to disavow the secret contradictory motives that kept drawing him to the forbidden city; but here Hannibal served him no better than Moses and actually confounded him, for in invoking a hero whose virtues were the exact opposite of his own he threw a glaring light on the problem of assimilation and betrayal which it was Hannibal's function to conceal.[39]

Yet Freud did not dwell for long on the heights to which Hannibal and Winckelmann had conspired to raise him; a more intimate memory soon brought him down, namely, the famous story of the "cap picked up out of the mud," which Jakob Freud had once told him to show how vastly the lot of the Jews had improved. This anecdote, with which his father had hoped to give him confidence in the future, had

completely missed its effect. The child had merely felt humiliated at having a father without character or courage, and
this was perhaps his first big disillusionment. "This struck me
as unheroic conduct on the part of the big, strong man who
was holding the little boy by the hand. I contrasted this situation with another which fitted my feelings better: the scene
in which Hannibal's father, Hamilcar Barca, made his boy
swear before the household altar to take vengeance on the
Romans. Ever since that time Hannibal had had a place in
my fantasies."[40] If he had to have a Jewish father, little Sigmund would at least have wanted him to be a man proud of
his race, a bold warrior, a heroic though vanquished Hamilcar, in whose footsteps he would be glad to follow. He too
would have liked to swear a solemn oath of vengeance,
which would give him an aim in life and at the same time
shield him from the inner dangers created by his insecure
position between two mutually hostile worlds. Instead of
which he had a weak father who, not content with swallow-
ing an insult and picking up his cap, made matters worse by
bringing up the incident years later by way of proving that
the times had changed for the better thanks to the new
liberalism of the Gentiles. The child never forgave him, and
his rancor was so deep-seated that traces of it were discernible many years later, when he was over forty, not only in
his dreams and fantasies, but also in the slips of his waking
life. In the first edition of the *Traumdeutung*, for example,
Freud called Hamilcar, Hannibal's father, Hasdrubal, which
is the name of one of Hannibal's brothers. Such a mistake
seems inconceivable in a man so well versed in ancient history, but it is easily explained. According to Freud's theory
of the unconscious determinism of our words and acts, these
slight disturbances in our mental functioning originate, like
dreams, in repressed desires. What then is the meaning of
this strange slip? "The error of putting Hasdrubal instead of
Hamilcar, the brother's name instead of the father's, occurred precisely in a context that concerned the Hannibal
fantasies of my school years and my dissatisfaction with my
father's behavior toward 'the enemies of our people.' I could

have gone on to tell how my relationship with my father was changed by a visit to England, which resulted in my getting to know my half-brother, the child of my father's first marriage, who lived there. My brother's eldest son is the same age as I am. Thus the relations between our ages were no hindrance to my fantasies of how different things would have been if I had been born the son not of my father but of my brother. These suppressed fantasies falsified the text of my book at the place where I broke off the analysis, by forcing me to put the brother's name for the father."[41]

Here we see that Freud's resentment was deeper and more lasting than it would appear from the *Traumdeutung;* otherwise, we should be at a loss to understand why as an adult he should still have been so disturbed by the memory of his father's story. But Jakob Freud's cowardice or opportunism in his relations with the "enemies of our people"[42] was not the only reason for his son's resentment; there were other reasons that appear clearly enough in his dreams over a period of several years, and some of them were so troubling that he was unable to speak of them openly. In the dream of the "botanical monograph," for example, his rivalry with Königstein and Koller in the matter of cocaine (he had written an article on coca which might have been termed a monograph) leads to his early passion for books and finally to a scene from his childhood in which his father handed him a book with color illustrations—probably to play with. From this graphically remembered scene we can infer that Jakob Freud was lacking in cultivation and refinement, that his approach to children was crude, to say the least, and that he regarded books (with the exception of the Bible) as so much paper. True, an incident of this kind might conceivably affect a child's idealized image of the paternal authority (sometimes less is needed to destroy that image completely); but after all, is it so grave, so painful, that a man of over forty should still relegate his memory of it to the realm of dreams? Yes, says Freud, but we are obliged to take his statement on faith, for once again his analysis is abridged; the very element that would have made it plausible is lacking: ". . . I can assure my readers that the ultimate meaning of the dream, which I have not disclosed, is intimately related to the subject of the childhood scene."[43] We are forced to conclude that the relatively harmless image of a father looking on while his children tear a book apart conceals a serious moral trauma; we cannot even guess at its nature, but it seems safe to say that at the time of writing Freud's resentment was still so intense that he shrank back from formulating it.

Another dream would probably have been more explicit if Freud had not taken care to curtail, or as he himself put it, to falsify his account of it—a deliberate deception which, as usual when he broke off the thread of his associations because they were leading him to denigrate his father, came to light in the end. The criticism that he withheld—in part no doubt because he regarded it as excessive and unjust—was revealed by one of those significant errors which he failed to detect in preparing the *Traumdeutung* for publication and which filled him with consternation later on.[44] This dream deals again with books and with another of Freud's misadventures in a train. It was dreamed in the course of a night journey. Freud enters a railway compartment occupied by a distinguished-looking couple, who despite their aristocratic appearance make no secret of their annoyance at his intrusion. These arrogant, disagreeable people, he says to himself, cannot have paid the full fare, and true enough, they were traveling on a free pass. As usual this privilege infuriates him. The woman is an imposing figure, a beauty on the decline. The man says nothing, and it is clear that he is not the dominant partner. All this makes a very unpleasant impression on Freud and he avenges himself in his dream by subjecting the disagreeable couple to all sorts of insults and humiliations. The dream itself is rather confused (true, the main part of it is not recorded); in it we find pell-mell: a place called "Hollthurn," where the train stops for ten minutes; holothurians (sea slugs); squatting women offering baskets of fruit for sale on the platform; another compartment, to which the dreamer somehow finds himself moved; an

English brother and sister; books lined up along a wall in such a way that Freud can read the English titles; he does not know whom they belong to, but the Englishman asks his sister if she hasn't forgotten a certain book by Schiller. The dreamer wakes up and ascertains that the train has stopped at Marburg. This is the censored text and there is no indication of where the falsification occurs. Where are we to look for it? We might logically suppose that it relates to the "primordial scene" so transparently evoked by the behavior of the real couple (the man and the woman representing parents furious at being disturbed during sexual intercourse, the intruder being of course their small child). But not at all; Freud does not sidestep this aspect of the "Oedipean" problem, though he attenuates its significance by telling us that he had taken one of his patients, a sufferer from obsessional neurosis, as his model. No, his secretiveness must relate to something else; in any event, to something that Freud has on his conscience, for it leads him to make a particularly troublesome slip, which soon afterward obliges him if not to lift the veil entirely, at least to admit that he has deliberately misrepresented the facts. After having identified the imaginary "Hollthurn" as the Marburg of his real journey, where the train actually stopped, Freud realized that the dream alluded to Schiller, since Schiller was born in Marburg. Freud was well aware, however, that Schiller was not born in Marburg but in Marbach; yet he made the mistake and allowed it to be printed. He corrected it only in the third edition, and then in a very succinct note: "This was one more of those mistakes which slip in as a substitute for an intentional falsification at some other point."[45] Here we discern a kind of law: every time Freud omits, deforms, or as here shamelessly falsifies a fact, in other words, every time he deceives the reader, he deceives himself elsewhere, as though to punish himself for his dishonesty. And amazingly enough, though these slips occur in different phases of his work, they all have the same significance: all "are products of repressed ideas relating to my late father."[46] In the Schiller-train dream, the text avenges itself for the falsification with a mistake related to the falsified content: "Anyone who reads through the dream analyzed on p. 266[47] [of the *Traumdeutung*] will in part find undisguisedly, and will in part be able to guess from hints, that I have broken off at thoughts which would have contained an unfriendly criticism of my father. In the continuation of this train of thoughts and memories there in fact lies an annoying story in which books play a part, and a business friend of my father's who bears the name of Marburg—the same name that woke me when it was called out at Marburg station on the southern railway. In the analysis I tried to suppress Herr Marburg from myself and from my readers; he took his revenge by intruding where he did not belong and changing the name of Schiller's birthplace from Marback to Marburg."[48] Since Herr Marburg never reappears in Freud's work, we have no way of knowing why Freud felt such an urgent need to suppress him. What crimes can he have committed? Had he been dishonest in business? Was he something of a crook, or merely imprudent like poor Uncle Josef? In *The Psychopathology of Everyday Life* Freud connects this mistake with a "disagreeable incident" in which books played a part (proof that there was something especially revolting in Jakob Freud's attitude toward books), but we do not know what books,[49] or whether it was these books that made Herr Marburg turn up so opportunely. We do know, however, that he was connected with a painful memory, with old resentments that welled up with undiminished force and that may not have been unfounded, since after all those years his mere association with Herr Marburg still cast such discredit on Jakob Freud that his son did his utmost to expel the matter from his thoughts.

Obviously we have no way of knowing how much truth there was in Sigmund's case against Jakob, but we do know that his dreams and fantasies were constructed almost methodically from a long list of real or imaginary, more or less explicit grievances. Attacks on Fliess and Breuer, disparagement of his Jewish colleagues considered as substitute fathers, anything could serve to consolidate his system of defense and to justify his thoughts of disavowal. Jakob is un-cultivated, he has no understanding whatever of what books mean to his son; he is cowardly "in the face of the enemies of our people"; he comes of a tainted family; he is closely connected, both in business and friendship with an unmentionable individual; in short, he is in every way disappointing, a far cry from the nobility and greatness that his son once imputed to him. Born a Jew by his father's fault, Sigmund finds himself in a situation of perpetual material and moral insecurity, torn between two communities, two cultures, two worlds of unequally favored memories, in constant danger of either betraying the cause of the people to which he is so devoted or of suffering vexations which are perhaps a prelude to an era of persecution.

During this period of inner crisis, sustained and in some measure aggravated by current events—the Dreyfus case in France, the slow rise of anti-Semitism in Austria—Freud's complaint against his father takes the form sometimes of relatively transparent accusations—delinquent brother; insane, epileptic, or feeble-minded nephews; lack of education; degrading connection with Herr Marburg; cowardice—and sometimes of more obscure recriminations. Thus, for example, he sees "a man standing on a cliff in the middle of the sea, in the style of Böcklin"; this man is himself, living in "splendid isolation" because of the boldness of his ideas, but he is also Dreyfus on Devil's Island, the dishonored, persecuted Jew, the victim of a monstrous injustice. In another dream he composes a lamentation in the biblical manner, into which he introduces the Yiddish word "*geseres*," which according to him means "weeping and wailing" (this is the sole example of a Yiddish word in his "fantasies"). "On account of events which had occurred in the city of Rome, it had become necessary to remove the children to safety, and this was done. The scene was then in front of a gateway, double doors in the ancient style (the 'Porta Romana' at Siena, as I was aware during the dream itself). I was sitting on the edge of a fountain and was greatly depressed and almost in tears. A female figure—an attendant or nun—

brought two boys and handed them over to their father, who was not myself. The elder of the two was clearly my eldest son; I did not see the other one's face. The woman who brought out the boy asked him to kiss her good-bye. She was noticeable for having a red nose. The boy refused to kiss her, but, holding out his hand in farewell, said '*Auf Geseres*' to her, and then '*Auf Ungeseres*' to the two of us (or to one of us). I had a notion that this last phrase denoted a preference."[50] The analysis of this dream and of the brief introductory dream consisting solely of a professor saying: "My son, the myops . . ."—leaves no doubt as to the typically Jewish situation already suggested by the manifest content of the vision. Freud had recently seen in Vienna a play entitled *The New Ghetto*,[51] which dealt with the Jewish question and, he tells us, revived his fears for the future of his children ("to whom one cannot give a country of their own"). In considering the segments of the dream one by one he thought of Exile—"By the rivers of Babylon there we sat down, yea, we wept"—and then of the absurd opposition *Geseres-Ungeseres*, corresponding to the significant opposition *gesäuert-ungesäuert* (leavened and unleavened), which evokes the Passover and the flight of the Jews from Egypt. Remembering that in the dream *Ungeseres* implies a preference, he suggests that in this part of the dream he sided entirely with the tradition. Thus the plaint of the Jewish father over his children indicates solidarity with the Jewish people in exile; here Rome is definitely the enemy, the Babylon excoriated by the prophets, and Freud has ceased to dream of going there to absorb its culture; he *is* there, but he is about to leave; the city drives him out and forces him to share the tragic fate of his brothers. The magical attraction of the Eternal City is dead; now the test of reality will begin.

Never has Freud seemed so close to his people as in this partly biblical sequence, but as usual the appearances are in some measure deceptive, for though he fully acknowledges his Jewishness, he does not cease to bemoan it, and his plaint is precisely the source of his dream; indeed, he complains bitterly and envies those who have had sufficient foresight to preserve their children from the perils of life as a Jew ("I was envying some relatives who, many years earlier, had had an opportunity of removing their children to another country"). But natural as they may be in a loving father, this complaint and this envy imply a reproach addressed to his own father, who simply "picked up his cap out of the mud" instead of taking action to provide his children with a more cheerful and less precarious future. In this respect Jakob Freud had been a "vague" father; he had chosen the shaky solution of pseudo-assimilation, which put his son in a false position just where he had the greatest need of stability and truth. Resigned, irresponsible, pusillanimous toward "the other side," he had doomed his children by leaving them no other possibility than submission to outward oppression or a shameful inner exile. And that was not all. The dreamer feared other evils than anti-Semitism. This he tells us in the four words—"My son, the myops"—that serve as a prologue to his dream. *Myops* makes him think of *cyclops*, a word used recently by Fliess in explaining his theory of bilaterality. The Cyclops with his one eye does not obey the laws of bilaterality (a criticism of Fliess); he is one-sided (*einseitig*). The words "my son the myops" express Freud's fear that his eldest son is intellectually as well as physically shortsighted, that he is stupid and backward. This accounts for the two symmetrically opposed formulas—*Auf Geseres/ Auf Ungeseres*—that replace the usual *Auf Wiedersehn* in the dream itself: by saying good-bye first on one side, then on the other, the son demonstrates his bilaterality, so showing that he is free from the dreaded family taint; the Jewish atavism has stopped with Freud's generation, so that Freud, encouraged in his hope of putting an end to the original sin of Jewishness, will never have to fear the terrible indictment he has leveled—not consciously, to be sure, but in the false innocence of his nights—against his own ancestors.

Thus beneath the obscure or transparent, sublime, or grotesque disguises favored by dreams, Jakob Freud is the true hero of the *Traumdeutung*, not a very heroic one to be sure, but tenderly loved and very much respected; revered, but hated as an obstacle and rival; worthy of pious affection and at the same time, because of the disappointing weakness the child has discovered in him, unworthy. He is a hero both cherished and detested, who secretly determines his son's extreme feelings—his emotional and intellectual enthusiasms, his passionate friendships strongly tinged with homosexuality, his propensity for transforming affection into aversion or hatred—for all the men with whom he was destined to be in any degree intimate.[52]

From the self-analysis that turned him into a ghost—not without reason, for it was his death that had made his son's self-analysis necessary and possible—Jakob Freud, or rather, his memory, derived a substantial benefit. Through it he ceased to be the corrupting and corrupt father whom Freud had long supposed to be at the source of all hysteria; he ceased to be the seducer of his own daughters, as his son, imprudently relying on the fables of his female hysteria patients, had believed for years. In 1893 he had indeed become convinced that all his hysteria patients had in childhood been seduced by their own fathers, or by some other father figure, and since then he had taken this belief as a law. And because this law, as he saw it, allowed of no exception, it necessarily compromised Jakob Freud, who thus became the seducer of his young daughters. But how could Sigmund Freud subscribe to such an absurdity? How could he bring himself to believe that all fathers lusted after their daughters and that none shrank back from the consequences of an incestuous act condemned by virtually all moral codes? True, when hysteria patients are encouraged to talk, they describe in endless detail the aggressions of which they claim to have been victims. But how could Freud, who was thoroughly familiar with their propensity for "displacing" the truth, believe such stories? He believed them because he needed them, because he needed a theory to justify his animosity toward Jakob and to help him misrepresent his fits of jealousy; and he was able to believe them because he was still far from suspecting that incestuous desires occur in the child and not in the parents—an insight that would oblige him not only to reject all the prevailing ideas about the innocence of childhood, but also to implicate himself in a very scabrous business. Rather than venture into such frightening territory, he clung to his patient's fables, at considerable loss to his therapy and to the development of his theory. It took his father's death and the psychic disorders it provoked in him to awaken him to the absurdity of his "law." At first he felt crushed; he saw the discovery from which he had expected so much reduced to nothing; he was over forty and this new failure after so many others seemed to dash his dearest hopes. But he did not give up, for he felt vaguely that in this game of hide-and-seek with the truth the mistake he had just detected might be the key to success.

As long as he believed in his patients' fantasies, he was unable to distinguish between the actual biographical facts dispersed throughout his material and the psychic reality which persisted in falsifying the facts; he mistook wish-fantasy for objective reality and duped by the everlasting delusions through which the human mind perpetuates its myths and superstitions, he became the accomplice of the patient's illness, hence powerless to cure it.

During the years when he persisted in believing the tendentious remarks of his patients, he seemed to be saying to himself and others: "No, I didn't lust after my mother, it was my father who lusted after my sisters," or: "No, I had no wicked feelings toward my father; it was he who condemned himself by his guilty designs on innocent children." This shifting of guilt, stemming directly from his neurosis, was responsible both for his therapeutic failures and for his failure to achieve social success. Consequently, he was paralyzed until he succeeded in setting things straight, in distinguishing truth from neurotic fiction, and in discerning the falsehood in the official version of reality. It may be said without exaggeration that psychoanalysis was born the day he discovered that those of his own dreams that he had analyzed contained no trace of a hysteria-provoking

father,[53] but that far from being a mirage pro-
v   by a deranged imagination, this mythical personage
derives his existence from very definite causes.

With his exposure of his hysteria patients' claim to have
been seduced in childhood, Freud had indeed penetrated to
the essence of his doctrine, and for the first time psychology
was in possession of a true precision instrument. For now he
knew the source of all beliefs in phenomena transcending experience, of all illusions concerning divine or supernatural
intervention in the lives of human beings; he knew the underlying cause of all superstitions and myths. He knew that
the human unconscious had the power to subjugate reason
and impose its wish fantasies by producing convincing
symptoms, and that nothing is more disastrous for the psychic and intellectual health of an individual than such a necessarily clandestine passage from *wish* to *accomplished fact*.
In thus exposing the principal ruse employed by the unconscious to achieve its ends, psychoanalysis defined its task,
which is: to distinguish as precisely as possible between pre-
dominantly unconscious psychic reality, which is all-powerful because it is not subject to the control of reason, and the
reality of shared experience, which is tangible, visible, and
subject to the principle of necessity. The essential aim of
analytic therapy and of the various applications of the psychoanalytic theory to history, sociology, and other realms of
knowledge, is to *analyze*, that is, to disjoin the two realms of
experience that the allied forces of neurosis and superstition
are perpetually confusing.

And this was also Freud's purpose when he began to analyze himself in earnest. Since his father was the main and
perhaps the only source of his psychic difficulties, it was
with his father that he had to begin; in other words, he had
to learn to distinguish the real Jakob Freud from the mythical father, upon whom all the son's most archaic impulses
had formerly been fixated, and whose multiple faces now be-
wildered him. If he succeeded, then Jakob Freud, at last dis-
sociated from his troublesome double, would cease to be the
inconceivable avatar of the Godhead or the diabolical

seducer, whose power of fascination was still felt by Sigmund Freud at the age of forty; and once brought down to earth, once he recovered his human form, he would take on the distinct features and infinitely varied nuances which are everywhere the mark of the living creature.

Freud's first attempt to effect this dissociation—in 1896 with the "You are requested to close the eyes" dream and the series of "Roman dreams"—does not seem to have brought him appreciably closer to his goal; for a time it even forced a retreat, for his self-analysis had so aggravated his disorder that he was obliged to break it off. But early in 1897 he resumed it (with the dream of "the uncle with the yellow beard"), and between June and September of the same year he plunged headlong into the adventure that was to carry him deep into the past in search of childhood memories, in which he now felt sure he would find the root of his strange disorder. By reconstructing the first three years of his life, he was able to form a clear picture of the "Oedipean" triangle; but though his science was saved by this enormous achievement, it brought no improvement to his private life. A mysterious taboo still forbade him to set foot in Rome, his scientific isolation was undiminished, and his dreams (e.g., "My son, the myops") still revolved around thoughts of death and exile. And so, after deciding to collect his analyses and work them into a book, he set bravely to work again, determined to rid himself of the last ghosts, which, though partly unmasked, still held him captive in their circle. And he soon found reason to hope for success, thanks to a decisive dream, which showed him exactly what he must do to regain his freedom.

At the time of the "Non vixit" dream—autumn 1898 —Freud was going through a period of profound depression. So great was his intellectual apathy that he almost abandoned the *Traumdeutung* (doubting his conclusions); he felt old, alone, feeble and listless, incapable, as he wrote to Fliess, of doing anything but "study the topography of Rome, my longing for which is becoming more and more acute . . ."[54] He continued to correspond actively with

Fliess, then his only friend, but his passion for that difficult man was beginning to take a new turn. His dreams revealed hostile feelings toward Fliess, and since he could not express such feelings in his letters, the letters became less frequent and much of what he did write seems insincere. Fliess at this particular time was both to be envied and pitied. His wife had just borne him a daughter, Pauline, a name that had been dear to Freud since his unspoken love for a sixteen-year-old girl by that name; but at the same time Fliess was so ill that those closest to him feared for his life. On October 16, 1898, Freud attended the unveiling of a bust of Professor Fleischl at the university; at this time he remembered that at his friend's funeral someone, shocked at the excessive praise of the deceased, had whispered: "No one is irreplaceable." Then a few days later, Freud had the dream that was to put an end to his old torments by showing him how to kill his ghosts.

This dream is more fantastic than most of Freud's dreams. Three beloved friends—Brücke, Ernst von Fleischl, and Josef Paneth—return from the dead; the fourth protagonist is a living man to whom Freud was very much attached, Fliess. It is night. Freud is in Brücke's laboratory, as in the days of his youth; he opens the door for Fleischl, who though dead sits quietly down at his desk. Freud knows that this is happening in July and that Fliess has come to Vienna without notifying him. He meets him on the street, in conversation with Joseph Paneth: "Fl. spoke about his sister and said that in three-quarters of an hour she was dead, and added some such words as 'that was the threshold.' As P. failed to understand him, Fl. turned to me and asked me how much I had told P. about his affairs. Whereupon, overcome by strange emotions, I tried to explain to Fl. that P. (could not understand anything at all, of course, because he) was not alive. But what I actually said—and I myself noticed the mistake—was '*Non vixit*.' I then gave P. a piercing look. Under my gaze he turned pale: his form grew indistinct and his eyes a sickly blue—and finally he melted away. I was highly delighted at this and I now realized that Ernst Fleischl, too, had been no more than an apparition, a *'revenant'*; and it seemed to me quite possible that people of that kind only existed as long as one liked and that one could get rid of them by wishing."[55]

Freud calls this dream a "fine specimen," a veritable compendium of the riddles characteristic of dreams; but to him it was also a source of embarrassment, for here again he could not tell all, but felt obliged to withhold a part of his findings, which deprived him of the satisfaction of providing tangible proof of his theory. "I would give a great deal," he wrote, "to be able to present the complete solution of its conundrums. But in point of fact I am incapable of doing so —of doing, that is to say, what I did in the dream, of sacrificing to my ambition people whom I greatly value. Any concealment, however, would destroy what I knew very well to be the dream's meaning . . ."[56] In this situation —eager to speak, but unable to tell the whole story—Freud resorts to a halfway measure: he provides partial information about the people whom he does not wish to sacrifice. Who are these people he loves but gravely offends in his dream? Of the four persons named in the text, only one is alive and as such entitled to be spoken of with a certain tact; that is Fliess, the friend concerning whom Freud has just received alarming news. In the dream this Fliess associates with ghosts; furthermore, he is designated by the letters Fl., which also stands for Fleischl. Thus Fliess is alive, but the dream kills him by lumping him together with three ghosts. Since at the time Freud thought Fliess's life was in danger, the wish for his friend's death implicit in the scenario seemed too revolting to speak of. Hence Freud's half-silence and his vague allusion to the "villainies" (this is where his phrase about the "unique villain" occurs) that the malignity of his dreams keeps forcing him to think up.

Among the selected themes that he consents to publish, we find: Brücke and his "terrible blue eyes"; Freud's habit of arriving late at the laboratory where the old master, a stickler for discipline, did not say a word but "overwhelmed" him with his terrible blue eyes; Fleischl and the bust bearing witness to his glory; the words *"Non vixit,"* spoken or rather seen in place of the NON VIVIT remembered from the inscription on the pedestal of the statue of the Emperor Josef at the Vienna Hofburg; *Josef* Paneth, whom Freud was thinking of at the time of the unveiling of the bust of Fleischl, regretting that he had died too young to earn a similar monument; July, the month of Julius Caesar, which leads to Shakespeare's *Julius Caesar* and Brutus, in whom Freud finds the best arguments with which to justify his own murderous desires; and finally a childhood memory, the memory of little John, his nephew, who was exactly the same age as himself and for whom he felt both passionate friendship and violent hostility. All the latent thoughts in this "fine specimen" converge on the same cluster of feelings and desires; with the megalomania characteristic of the dreamer, Freud endows himself with the attributes of old Brücke, the venerable master of his younger days, whom he still regarded as the supreme authority; thus metamorphosed, he is able to "overwhelm" his friend Josef Paneth with a look to punish him for once having wished for the death of Fleischl, their common friend, who was an obstacle to his advancement. On this point, however, Freud is no better than Josef, for he too has desired the death of that hero of science, that "Greek god," for whom he felt as much envy as admiration; he has indeed desired it consciously, and for the same reason, because it would have opened the road to his own advancement. Directed as it was against a man condemned, as Freud knew, to die soon, and whose death he had reason to believe he had hastened (by giving him cocaine to break the morphine habit), such a base and needlessly cruel wish should have redoubled Freud's sense of guilt; the punishment, however, falls not on Freud, but on Paneth, who in the dream is declared to be nonexistent (*Non vixit*). With this Freud is rid of the remorse that has long been tormenting him over the numerous murders he has committed in the course of his nights or in the penumbra of his daydreams. His brother Julius had died as Freud had wished (here he makes no mention of this brother, but it seems only natural to associate "Julius" with Julius Caesar and July); Fleischl and Paneth have also died as a result of his wishes, and Fliess will soon incur the same fate, for he has now become the butt of Freud's malignant wishes. But far from being distressed at having so brutally eliminated all those who stood in his way, he is "highly delighted"; he even takes pride in being still alive while so many of those around him have fallen by the wayside, and what makes this pride all the greater is his awareness of having killed his rivals by the sheer force of desire, thanks to the magic power deriving from the omnipotence of thought.

One might have expected Jakob Freud to appear among all these men whom the dreamer causes at will to die, to return to life and to die again, or at least expected the interpreter of the dream to remark on his absence. Was he not the earliest of Sigmund's ghosts, the closest to him, and by far the most damning? Undoubtedly, and it is to him that the analysis should logically lead, if the chain of associations had not been broken off in time, the analysis must logically have led to him. The whole "Non vixit" dream revolves around the father-phantom, whose last vestige the son had to kill if he was to live in freedom. Of this Freud was well aware, but the thought of avowing his "posthumous parricide" was so repellent to him that he preferred to pass over in silence everything that might have led up to it. And as usual he paid for his bad faith with a significant slip. And this time his mistake escaped him so totally that he was unable to retrieve himself by analyzing it after the fact: it remained in the text of his analysis until someone else—again Fritz Wittels, the "unsolicited biographer"—came along and corrected it.[57]

For saying *Non vixit* in his dream instead of the *Non vivit* required by the situation was not Freud's only mistake; he compounded it in the waking state by misquoting the inscription on the pedestal of the emperor's statue. It actually runs:

Saluti publicae vixit
Non diu sed totus.

Freud substitutes *patriae* for *publicae*, as though the devil had moved him to bring back the father-phantom he had wanted to exorcise. Starting with this misquotation, the sequence of ideas takes on a coherent meaning in which death and fame are closely linked. It is because he was the leader and father of his country that the Emperor Josef has his statue in the Hofburg; the same goes for Fleischl, a bust of whom has been set up in the university, and for Paneth, who also would have had his bust if the world had had time to recognize his genius; and of course for Jakob Freud, to whom in the *Traumdeutung* his son erects a monument, a highly ambivalent one, to be sure, but still a monument, erected in a sincere impulse of piety to perpetuate his memory. In the dream, however, the monument signifies not only death as the end of life; the mistaken *Non vixit* suggests rather that the monument is a mark of nullity: for all their glory, these statued individuals never existed in reality, they are nonentities in the strict sense of the word, and the dreamer who possesses glory only in his imagination can indulge in the pleasure of sending time back to nothingness.

The "Non vixit" dream teaches this truth: ghosts are nothing in themselves; they cannot torment everyone, but only the soul that is too weak, too fainthearted to surmount his remorse, and they vanish as soon as one looks at them with clear, unflinching eyes. From this dream psychoanalysis, which is at bottom nothing other than the art of dispelling the phantasmagorias of the psyche, derived a sound principle and the substance of its future reflections. But what of Freud himself in the conduct of his life? Was he now to draw a sharp dividing line between Jakob Freud and the figment he had devised long ago to compensate for his obscure birth and avenge himself on authority? Had he penetrated deeply enough into the unconscious causes of his guilt feelings to safeguard him against future enchantments? Would his real father, whom despite his resentment he had not ceased to love, at last be able to protect him from the phantom-father whom he had fabricated in order to be able to express his remorse, his jealousy and his frantic ambition with impunity? In short, could he now regard himself as cured? The "Non vixit" dream had indeed provided him with a formula for cure—". . . people of that kind only existed as long as one liked"—but this dream was not by any means the last in the series; the *Traumdeutung* contains others in which Jakob Freud undergoes all sorts of ambivalent metamorphoses.[58] His occult presence was indeed remarkably tenacious; not only did he exert a subterranean influence on the more or less novelistic part of his son's work—*Totem and Taboo, Moses and Monotheism;* he also continued to intervene not infrequently in his son's life by bringing the full weight of an importunate past to bear on the present. Undoubtedly he was in some measure responsible for the alternation of infatuation and disaffection in so many of Freud's friendships and for his ambivalent—now active, now passive—role in the quarrels and conflicts which were soon to break out in the Psychoanalytic movement and which, by maintaining a state of permanent petty warfare around him, sometimes left him unhappier and more isolated than he had been in his previous obscurity. No, Freud did not rid himself of his ghosts as fully as he chose to believe when he analyzed his "Non vixit" dream; at fifty he was still haunted, so much so that when he came to satisfy his second great desire, there was his father back again, reproaching him as usual for indulging his fancies and for having betrayed him by succeeding too well in life. The memory of the malaise that made him doubt the reality of the Acropolis[59] remained an inexplicable torment, and for more than thirty years he looked for the key to this last magic spell. For neither the apathy of old age nor the suffering due to his terrible illness, nor the terrors attendant on the rise of Nazism could overcome his passionate curiosity concerning everything connected with his father. When at last he found Jakob Freud behind his famous "disturbance of memory," he felt only tenderness, piety, and perhaps pity for his father as well as regret at not having always been able to love him. True, at the end of his career the thought that he, the son, had achieved "superiority" still gave him feelings of remorse; he could not forgive himself for having become famous, though late and at great cost; he had not wholly overcome the impure and excessive feelings that made his filial tenderness an intolerably violent passion. But he could justly say to himself that on one point at least he had not weakened: if he had not avenged his father as he had sworn to by following in the footsteps of Hannibal, neither had Rome vanquished him; he had not succumbed to the spells of the mythical city, which for him was the symbol of ambition and disavowal. He had destroyed the city in his own way, by destroying the tissue of illusory images that transformed it into an inviolable site, sacred in the twofold ancient sense of the word, that is, holy, forbidden to the profane and protected by a mortal taboo.

This victory over his personal myth, which marks not only the end of the century but also a new era in the history of thought, gave him the certainty that he could now win a leading position "on the other side" without fear of disavowing himself; that he could go to Rome and admire everything he loved there without feeling even in his dreams, even for the time of the most fleeting dream, the slightest temptation to bend his knee.

V

THE LAST NOVEL

Thanks to his self-analysis, which showed him the ambivalence of his relations with his father and the contradictory nature of his Jewish sentiment, Freud was able to go his own way, which was neither a withdrawal into the Jewish world nor the disavowal that is more or less implicit in assimilation. For now he knew that what he found within himself in the course of his adventurous journey was present in every man, regardless of the factors of time, place, race, and culture that determine the visible part of the personality. In writing to Fliess in 1897: "I found that I too had been in love with my mother and jealous of my father . . ."[1] Freud implied that his own experience had merely confirmed a clinical fact that was already known to him, but this was hardly the case. What he found in himself by analyzing his dreams was not at all what he expected—"the early seduction of hysteria patients"—but something absolutely unheard of, which obliged him to retrace his steps and revise his whole theory. Once the analytic understanding of his own case had given him the means of rectifying the error that had long been impeding his progress, he was finally able to understand the inner life of his patients and then, on the strength of abundant clinical data, to formulate a law valid for all mankind. The "Oedipus complex"—the infant's desire for the parent of opposite sex and hatred of the other parent seen as a rival to be eliminated—had ceased to be a pathological accident and became a universally human fatality, or more precisely *the* human fatality par excellence. Now Freud, who by scrutinizing the Jewish drama of his childhood had reconstituted the drama of all childhood, might legitimately have said to the Gerstäckers and Lasemanns who asked him to become like them, to cast off his innermost self and make himself acceptable to them: "I am not like you and never will be. To tell the truth, I have no reason to want to resemble you, for in a profound sense that you do not even suspect, *it is you who are like me*, potential parricides and incestuous sons. I have found this out by hard experience, and if not for me you would never have known it. Accordingly, it is I who call on you to 'assimilate' by discovering what you really are." Obviously no such words—implicit in Freud's work—will be spoken for many years; serious people will laugh at this "old wives' tale" for a long time to come. Nevertheless, once the *Traumdeutung* was published, the situation in regard to assimilation underwent a historic change; psychoanalysis had built a bridge to "the other side," a solid bridge which was its work from end to end, and from then on it was psychoanalysis, a Jewish science, that would provide the basis for communication between the two sides.

Thus psychoanalysis offers more than communication between consciousness and the unconscious part of the psyche; it also serves as an intermediary between two forms of culture and thought, not like other Jewish movements by inclining to the norms of the dominant society, but by establishing a distinct and independent order of knowledge, which breaks radically with the religious and philosophical tradition of the West. Outside of this order, in which the known and the unknown are continually changing places, man, whether sick or sound, will be at the mercy of occult psychic forces whose existence he is obliged to deny, and he will never attain sufficient knowledge of himself to make him in any degree master of his fate. Anyone wishing to dispel the old phantoms and transcend the narrow limits of the old official knowledge will henceforth be constrained to espouse the new law, which denounces the old one or at least declares it obsolete. And whenever Western civilization, alarmed at its hidden undercurrents, is impelled to question its spiritual infrastructures, it will have to do likewise.

Of course this reversal of the situation was not exactly an event; or if it was, then only in the extreme subjectivity of a Freud engaged in interpreting his dreams and phantasms. While subjectively he had every reason to regard himself as the man whom "the other side" needed, who would help "the others" overcome their blindness, objectively he could not prevent his work from being looked upon as a perfect example of assimilation, as the product of a deeply absorbed culture, and this it undoubtedly was. For while psychoanalysis has retained next to nothing of the typically Jewish situation that gave it its first impetus, it invokes a wide range of learned or popular notions gathered from the common fund of European culture; moreover, it derives certain of its essential concepts from literature and mythology, as though wishing not only to make itself understood by a select public, but also to flaunt the extent of its borrowings. In this connection the term "Oedipus complex" is sufficiently revealing, though it did not actually originate with Freud,[2] and it is by no means the only psychoanalytic term marking a cultural synthesis. Psychoanalysis has drawn its terms and concepts from any number of sources, and in this it reflects its founder's feelings of friendship and admiration for many masters in many fields. Nevertheless, its dependence on "the other side" relates far less to the present than to the historic past: it works with reminiscences taken over from Gentile culture, but its message to modern man consists exclusively in its way of explaining the human mind, and that is entirely its own.[3] Because of its theory of the unconscious, which obliges it to investigate phenomena that the sciences, religions, and philosophies have always excluded from their field of vision, and to attach extreme importance to what other disciplines have disregarded, psychoanalysis can claim to rest entirely on its own feet, to be its own law and criterion of truth. Radically independent—it is not a prolongation of any other discipline and requires no outside help for its development—it is for every disciple and every patient, regardless of intellectual horizon, an absolute beginning.

After a period of being limited to the Vienna Psycho-analytical Society where, as Freud himself put it, it was in danger of becoming a "Jewish national affair," the movement spread abroad, arousing such enthusiasm in men already prominent in their own countries that not a few of them were willing to endanger their material security and reputation for the cause. The first foreign recruits were Swiss, the most eminent among them being the psychiatrists Bleuler, Jung, and Binswanger, and the Protestant clergyman Oskar Pfister. The enthusiasm of such men seems all the more remarkable when we consider that nothing in their education had prepared them for such a revolution. In this respect the Jews gathered around Freud in his Viennese "ghetto" had had no great difficulty; the inventor of psychoanalysis spoke as it were in their name; they followed him instinctively and did not feel too lost ("It is easier for us Jews"). It was a very different matter with the Swiss, a change from one world to another. They had to rid themselves of beliefs, habits of thought, and prejudices of all kinds inherent in their background, to which they were still very much attached even when they thought themselves fully emancipated. Since such imponderables exert a determining influence and are almost impossible to get rid of, the new adepts were under constant temptation to adapt Freudian psychoanalysis to the traditions of a more or less secularized Christianity. Thus their entry into the movement soon provoked conflicts, or more precisely, misunderstandings which Freud had to rectify at every turn if he was not to see his doctrine corrupted for the benefit of old religious attitudes.

It was doubtless in the very nature of the psychoanalytic movement to be constantly shaken by quarrels and dissensions. Freud was the "father," and since few of his early pupils had been properly analyzed, if at all, he became the victim of the father complexes which they accused one another of not having been able to resolve. Thus the most trifling theoretical argument degenerated into a passionate quarrel.

In this small group united by the strangest of callings, hostilities originated at least as much in personal animosities and jealousies as in purely doctrinal divergencies. This was one of the reasons why Freud felt so ill at ease in the Vienna group; another was the uncontrollable antipathy he felt for the personality, character, and manners of certain Viennese members. ("Did you ever see the likes of that gang?" he is quoted as having said to Lionel Binswanger as they were leaving a meeting of the association together.[4]) He disliked Adler, Stekel, and Tausk, and his aversion must have had a good deal to do with the squabbles that threatened the unity of the movement from the very start. Tausk killed himself for reasons that had nothing to do with theory; Stekel propounded his own "science of dreams," full of the extravagant notions that Freud had managed to avoid; and Adler honestly admitted, privately if not in his writings, that he broke with Freud chiefly because he could not bear the thought of spending the rest of his life in the shadow of the great man.[5] Of course personal grudges were not the whole story. Among those men who had been brought together by their unhappiness rather than by their affinities, there were real differences in outlook which would have created conflicts sooner or later in any event. But serious as were the deviations of a Stekel or an Adler—and serious they were, especially in Adler's case, insofar as they represented a step back in the direction of the old psychology—in one respect at least these men respected the essence of psychoanalysis: they did nothing to restore the obsolete idols, the transcendent values of ethics, religion, and philosophy, in short, the "illusions" which Freud had dispelled.

It was a very different matter with the disciples in other countries—especially the Swiss and the Americans—who came to psychoanalysis with little knowledge of its inner workings and deeper implications. Attracted by the miraculous, for which the *Traumdeutung* seemed to offer new possibilities and—in this century of "narrow-minded" rationalism—an unhoped-for theoretical underpinning; despite all arguments to the contrary, still deeply attached to the ethical and philosophical assumptions of the society in which they lived, these men, who brought to Freud their militant enthusiasm and the weight of their authority, were victims from the start of a grave misunderstanding: they expected psychoanalysis not to *disenchant* them—its proper function —but on the contrary to "enchant" them a little more by bolstering up their "illusions" with a brand-new scientific authority. The *Traumdeutung* offered spectacular proof of the existence between heaven and earth of innumerable things which contemporary positivist science, imprisoned in its own rigid rules, could only declare to be nonexistent or at best outside its field of vision. All those who rejected official science because it took no interest in their anguished questions about life, death, the mystery of man, and ultimate ends, rallied to the heretical Jewish science which seemed, by rehabilitating the *soul,* to bridge the gap between the hallowed old wisdoms and the most advanced modern science. A product of science but hostile to the prejudices of official science; analytical but diametrically opposed to the analytical spirit inherent in the skepticism of the day, psychoanalysis became for many the exemplary science which by finally resolving all false antinomies boldly opened the road to a new alchemy.

The genius of Freud discovered an aspect of man's relations with himself and the world that had hitherto been perceived only by poets and mystics. The next step was to reconcile this revolutionary vision with the lofty values implicit in our cultural superstructures. Psychoanalysis had shown that children possessed an apparently innate gift of "godmaking," that they spontaneously deify everything that seems great, endowed with mysterious power, beyond their understanding. Might one not infer from this a religious "instinct," which would at last provide a scientific justification of the revealed religions? And similarly might there not be an ethical "instinct" and another, no less compelling, tending toward the true, the pure and the beautiful? And since the unconscious can be equated with the occult, might one not use it to establish a science of the irrational, thus making all so-called superstitions and irrational beliefs objects of serious investigation? Since—as had now been irrefutably proved—dreams and hallucinations have meaning despite their apparent absurdity, might one not with their help retrieve the element of truth contained in the various forms of mysticism? Did Freudian determinism not argue in favor of the philosophical finalism that had been so discredited by modern thought? And finally, could psychoanalysis not be expected to effect a vast synthesis of all modes of knowledge, leading to a reconciliation between science on the one hand and religion and philosophy on the other? For some fifteen years—roughly up to the time of the First World War—disputes between Freud and his non-Austrian disciples revolved around such efforts to rehabilitate the cultural "values" and the finality of thought. Some of the controversies resulted in spectacular breaks—as was soon the case with Bleuler and some years later with Jung. Other friendships were unaffected—Freud never quarreled with Pfister or Binswanger, though their views on these matters were far removed from his. But all these men—the spiritualist psychiatrists of the Burghölzli, the Protestant pastor, the American moralist James Putnam—had one thing in common: they were repelled by the thought of explaining the high by the low, of reducing the sublime to instinct, in short, by analysis in the strict sense of the word, and here Freud could make no concessions without destroying his most precious creation with his own hands.[6]

In his written or spoken answers to the "ultimate" questions with which he was assailed at that time, we find not a single word to suggest that he ever wavered on this point. "*Men,*" he said one day to Binswanger, "*have always known they had spirit; it was for me to show them that they also had instincts.* But men are always dissatisfied; they can't wait, they must always have something finished or complete . . ."[7] To the same friend, who for years urged him to add something to his doctrine that would meet his own, Binswanger's, philosophical needs, Freud addressed a profession of faith, or rather non-faith, which perfectly sums up his views in the matter: "I have always lived on the ground floor and in the basement of the building—you maintain that on changing one's viewpoint one can also see an upper floor housing such distinguished guests as religion, art, and others. You are not the only one; most cultivated specimens of *homo natura* think likewise. In this respect you are the conservative, I the revolutionary. If I had another life of work ahead of me, I would dare to offer even those high-born people a home in my lowly hut. I already found one for religion when I stumbled on the category 'neurosis of mankind.' But we are probably talking at cross purposes and it will be centuries before our dispute is settled."[8] At the age of eighty, of course, Freud had little hope of convincing those of his disciples who, dazzled by his genius but impervious to his teaching, wished at all costs to project upon the heavens what he had laboriously discovered in his basement. But to the end he persevered in what he knew to be his revolutionary position. He had come to bury the gods and idols whose dying cult still obscured the perspectives of thought, and in this salutary task only people patient and humble enough to exclude heaven from their preoccupations could help him.

During the forty-odd years of his leadership over the movement he had founded, Freud never ceased to struggle against all attempts to blunt or eliminate the sharpest thorns in his work. He thought of himself as destined to "destroy the peace of the world,"[9] and in his eyes the mission of psychoanalysis is not to subordinate itself to the recognized values of Western thought, but to declare war on mental laziness in all its forms, the most pernicious being the recourse to eternal "values."

In continually disturbing the civilized world by the critical examination of its sublimities, Freud defeated the Rome of his dreams and this unprecedented victory consoled him amply for his failure to take the warlike path of Hannibal. He avenged his father, himself, and his people—in a most unusual way, but so completely and brilliantly that he had every reason to feel that he had discharged his oath and eradicated the last traces of his guilt. And yet, as his late work shows, he had not gained peace; to the very end he remained the transgressor, the tormented, tormenting, haunted son, whose only surcease lay in continually renewing the old mystery of his remorse. Not that Freud pursued the confession he had once succeeded in making under cover of the *Traumdeutung;* from then on he was careful not to speak of himself, and his confessions were in a sense impersonal, implied in the obsessive recurrence of certain themes —revolt of the sons, murder of the father, the endless chain of crime and expiation, and still more perhaps in his doubts as an author, the misgivings and hesitations that inexplicably delayed the publication of his work.

In point of fact, Freud was far from feeling the same about all his works. Regardless of the outcry that was to be feared from the representatives of official science or conformist morality, he had no qualms at all about his purely scientific works. But whenever a disguised autobiography was involved—chiefly in his attempts at applied psychoanalysis—he suffered a strange malaise. The writing itself gave him unaccustomed difficulties, and once the work was finished, he was assailed by doubts and misgivings that made him keep postponing publication. In 1912, for example, it took the concerted efforts of his pupils to overcome his unwillingness to publish *Totem and Taboo*[10]; in 1914 it was only under the cover of anonymity that he could bring himself to publish his essay "The *Moses* of Michelangelo"; and twenty years later he released his other *Moses* bit by bit, reluctantly, accompanying each installment with embarrassed explanations that show how uncomfortable he must have felt. The central theme of *Totem and Taboo* is the historical murder of the original father by his sons; *Moses and Monotheism* takes up the same theme, no longer applied to the nameless father of the primitive clan, but to the Jewish father murdered at the dawn of our history and civilization. On the face of it Freud wrote "The *Moses* of Michelangelo" as an attempt to solve certain problems attaching to the famous statue. His real motives, however, are made clear from the start, for the Moses he describes tends to keep stepping out of the marble and coming to life like the Commander in the last act of *Don Giovanni*, threatening to seize his sacrilegious murderer in his terrible stone fist. Thus, in all three cases, the "Oedipean" drama, which at the time of the *Traumdeutung* was merely an expression of infantile desires that could not be fulfilled, became the monstrous reality at the base of all history, the immense crisis, fraught at once with crimes and with progress, by which Freud himself, for all his science, was still literally shaken.[11]

"The *Moses* of Michelangelo" differs from all Freud's other works in one respect: in it he speaks very little of psychoanalysis as such. It is the work, the anonymous author tells us, of a simple art lover who happens to be acquainted with some psychoanalysts and, having acquired a smattering of their science, ventures to say a few words, amusing perhaps but without scientific ambition, about "the crown of modern sculpture," as Hermann Grimm called the statue in question. Of course it would never have occurred to him to write such a paper if the statue hadn't meant a great deal to him, but he wishes to repeat that he is a mere amateur, implying that his amateur status is his reason for withholding his name.[12]

To Freud, however, this *Moses* was far from being one masterpiece among others. For one thing, it was closely connected with Rome and the papacy, both of which, as we have seen, had played a determining role in the secret economy of his ambitions. Furthermore, his relationship with this statue was truly extraordinary, and quite irrationally he believed it to be reciprocal. Now that he was able to visit Rome, he went to see the marble colossus on each one of his trips, and it had become thoroughly familiar to him. Nevertheless, the sight of it, inspiring a mixture of admiration and terror, was almost more than he could bear, and he sometimes fled, as though fearing that the statue would suddenly come to life: "How often have I mounted the steep steps from the unlovely Corso Cavour to the lonely piazza where the deserted church stands, and have essayed to support the angry scorn of the hero's glance! Sometimes I have crept cautiously out of the half-gloom of the interior as though I myself belonged to the mob upon whom his eye is turned—the mob which can hold fast no conviction, which has neither faith nor patience, and which rejoices when it has regained its illusory idols."[13] Here Freud, ordinarily so reserved about his inner life, exposes himself without the slightest need, or rather because of an imperious psychic need, and makes the most incredible of confessions. At the age of fifty-eight, he behaved like a child in the presence of the statue, he was afraid of the stone hero, at once hoping and fearing that it would come to life: "I can recollect my own disillusionment when, during my first visits to San Pietro in Vincoli, I used to sit down in front of the statue in the expectation that I should now see it start up on its raised foot, dash the Tables of the Law to the ground and let fly its wrath. Nothing of the kind happened . . . Instead, the stone image became more and more transfixed, an almost oppressively solemn calm emanated from it, and I was obliged to realize that something changeless was here represented; that this Moses would remain sitting like this in his wrath for ever."[14] One can hardly doubt that the scene here described was experienced many times in a kind of sacred terror and that the true subject of the essay was not so much Michelangelo's statue as the living man it purports to represent, the man Moses, father of the Jews and eternally offended Jewish father, before whom Freud felt himself to be eternally at fault. For to experience so unreasonable a fear —he always tried "to support the angry scorn of the hero's glance" but sometimes fled defeated, as though really in fear of bodily chastisement—he must have had reasons for feeling guilty, not in general, because of vague thoughts and past failings, but there and then, at that particular moment, face to face with that block of marble suddenly transformed into an implacable judge. Moses would punish him, because he, Freud, belonged to the "mob which can hold fast to no conviction, which has neither faith nor patience, and which rejoices when it has regained its illusory idols." Like them, he was vacillating, impatient for immediate happiness, an idolater and apostate; he merited the punishment meted out to the Jews; the drama of Mount Sinai would be repeated for his benefit; once again the Tables of the Law would be shattered and the old Jewish tragedy would be re-enacted at the expense of the present-day sinner most worthy of it. For if Freud felt insignificant in the presence of the Titan, he felt magnified by the greatness of his sin, which in itself justified all the grandeur of the drama. And despite his fear of punishment, or perhaps because of it, he wished to suffer the rigors of the Law immediately, to have done with his anguished waiting. But he was disappointed: nothing happened, Moses did not move, he "would remain sitting like this in his wrath for ever," and face to face with the image of the petrified father, the dead father whose anger would never be appeased, Freud learned once again that he was doomed to bear all the weight of his guilt alone.

Since the art lover who claimed authorship of the essay was supposed to have only slight knowledge of psychoanalysis, he could hardly have dwelt on the content of this guilt without unmasking himself. Yet by identifying himself with the faithless "mob," he suggests that it has to do with the disavowal of his father and origins, that burning theme in which so many unconscious currents converged. And this idea is reinforced by the association of Rome with Moses, which closely resembles his old vision of the Promised Land, with the difference that here the connection is more concrete, for Michelangelo's Moses *is* in Rome and was conceived as part of the tomb that Michelangelo had been commissioned to erect for one of the greatest of the popes. Here phantasm, dream, and fiction were replaced by tangible reality: having definitely overcome his Roman inhibition, Freud was really in Rome; he was really looking at the statue; he really became afraid of it every time he looked at it, and he really expected it to spring to its feet. Freud's strange state of mind in San Pietro dei Vincoli cannot be equated with a mere daydream. For one thing, it recurred regularly, and moreover its effect on Freud was so powerful as to set his body in motion. (He cautiously recoils from the sacred anger of that marble gaze.) So striking an effect would seem to warrant a few words of explanation, but Freud does not see fit to explain; his strange relationship with the statue serves solely as an introduction to the main body of the article, devoted to the ambiguity of the statue's gestures, which are not in agreement with the scene described in the Bible.[15] Thus the story is left hanging in mid-air. The narrator breaks off at the moment when the hallucination ceases: the hero who is on the point of returning to life to judge him is summarily sent back to his eternity.

Thus for the moment Moses returned to the inert matter from which he had almost escaped, and Freud, suffering from remorse but spared his punishment, remained very much alive in face of the Titan reduced to immobility. But this was not the end of the matter, for twenty years later the story of the immolated Jewish father was resumed, and Freud reconstituted all the details in a story that is both impersonal and passionate and may be regarded as the final chapter of his novel. It is the same story, but in a very different variant, for the Moses who captivated him at the very end was no longer the sculptured image whose power left him crushed, but the great sculptor of men who had changed the destiny of mankind.

It is perhaps no accident that Moses renewed his hold on Freud in the last years of his life, at a time when, beset by illness and grief, disappointed in his affection for certain of his disciples and afflicted by the loss of those closest to him —Abraham had died in 1925 and Ferenczi in 1933—he was obliged to look on as a tidal wave of barbarism threatened to carry away everything that was dear to him. To the infirmities of age and the physical torment he had endured patiently for more than ten years (cancer of the jaw) was now added the German catastrophe of 1933, with its threat not only to himself and his family, but also to the cause of science and truth. Austria was spared for the moment, but the pressure of Nazi Germany was felt from the first, and the worst was to be feared in the not too distant future. Even if Freud were not personally in danger for the moment, he knew that if the new blood-myth were to triumph in his country he would have little reason to want to go on living. A few months after Hitler's seizure of power, he wrote to Oskar Pfister: "Our horizon has become darkly clouded by the events in Germany . . . My judgment of human nature, above all the Christian-Aryan variety, has had little reason to change."[16] But the brutal irruption of archaic forces, which had supposedly been laid to rest long ago, not only reinforced his native pessimism but reopened the old wound of Jewish existence and the fundamental question of his origins, which no amount of historical knowledge could solve. "Faced with the renewed persecutions," he wrote to Arnold Zweig, "one asks oneself again how the Jew came to be what he is and why he has drawn upon himself this undying hatred."[17] Thus for Freud, Nazism was not as for a Marxist primarily the spearhead of a social and political reaction whose causes are at least in part accessible to analysis; nor was it solely an outburst of savagery that a European humanist could view from outside, without at all questioning the principles of his own civilization; it was also a *trial* in the traditional sense of the word, a tribulation compelling a Jew to meditate on himself and the stumbling block of his singularity. For where others can take sides with a clear conscience on the strength of their enlightened opinions, a Jew must first put himself to the test, must first look not among his persecutors but within himself and in the dense texture of his own millennial history, for the explanation of the millennial hatred that his race has brought upon itself by the mere fact of its existence. Consequently, instead of asking himself how the Germans had become what they were in 1933, how it had been possible for highly cultivated people to arrive at such a degree of abasement, Freud questioned himself about the "mysterious thing that makes the Jew,"[18] and why it aroused such deep-seated hatred in the majority.

He questioned himself, but actually, when he spoke of it to Arnold Zweig, he already had his solution and if we are to take him at his word he had discovered it without much difficulty: "I soon found the formula: Moses created the Jew. And my essay received the title: *The Man Moses, a Historical Novel* (with more right than your novel about Nietzsche). The material is divided into three parts: the first reads like an interesting novel; the second is laborious and lengthy; the third substantial and exacting. The enterprise foundered on the third section, for it contains a theory of religion which, although nothing new to me after *Totem and Taboo*, is nevertheless bound to be something fundamentally new and shattering to the uninitiated. Concern for these uninitiated compels me to keep the completed essay secret."[19] According to this extraordinary "historical novel," the key to the Jewish enigma was to be sought in the man Moses. The book was ready for the printer in September 1934, but Freud could not bring himself to publish it; for a strange mixture of reasons, which he divulged later on along with his discoveries, he withheld the manuscript, but was able neither to reject it entirely nor to rework it. When he finally decided to publish it, he did so chapter by chapter, perhaps as much to cushion his own shock at seeing it in print as to spare the public.[20]

One of the reasons given by Freud—both in his correspondence and in the body of the work—for delaying publication of the essay was political. It does not seem unfounded, for the clerical, Christian-Social regime then in power was hardly favorable to daring ideas, and the learned Father Schmidt, known to be an unofficial agent of the Vatican, was at the height of his influence. Unfortunately for Freud, this Father Schmidt (who had collaborated with Andrew Lang in formulating the theory of "original monotheism") had expressed bitter hostility to *Totem and Taboo*, and there was no reason to believe that he would be less so to the *Moses*, which was merely an application of the same general idea to the special case of the Jews. Freud thought it wiser not to defy him too openly and to wait for events, good or bad, that might leave him free to speak.[21]

His main concern was not for himself. What worried him

most was that the rise of fascism might seriously damage the psychoanalytic movement, and that his disciples in some countries might suddenly be deprived of their living. The young Italian Society was already having serious difficulties with the Vatican, and if not for the friendship between Edoardo Weiss, its founder, and Mussolini, it would probably have been suppressed. Under such conditions it would have been irresponsible on Freud's part to defy the Austrian government. And then came an unforeseen, not to say paradoxical, development that robbed him of all desire to antagonize the clergy. Reacting against triumphant Nazism, the Catholic Church, abandoning for once its traditional policy of supporting the regime in power, seemed determined to resist Nazi terror and defend the cause of freedom (though two years later, as Freud observed with bitterness, its traditions regained the upper hand). In 1934 the anxious Austrian Jews could still hope to find a last protector in the Church, and to Freud this was one more reason for leaving Moses in abeyance.

Undoubtedly political considerations had a good deal to do with this temporization, for in 1939, after the psychoanalytic societies had been dissolved in the Greater Reich and he himself had emigrated, he finally published the book in its entirety, without regard for the feelings of religious believers. Furthermore, the prospect of seeing the book maliciously attacked and quite possibly suppressed cannot have been very attractive to a man of eighty. But he also had other reasons for withholding publication. He had his doubts about the value of his work. "In addition to all this," he wrote in the same letter to Arnold Zweig, "there is the feeling that the essay doesn't seem to me too well substantiated, nor do I like it entirely. So all in all it would be a risk to get my *Moses* published. But the risk, though real enough, is not the only obstacle. More important is the fact that this historical novel won't stand up to my own criticism. I need more certainty and I should not like to endanger the final formula of the whole book, which I regard as valuable, by founding it on a base of clay."[22] Between 1934 and 1936—and even after the first two chapters of the book had appeared—statements of this kind recur frequently in Freud's letters to his closest friends. In this there is nothing very new; he was usually depressed after completing an important work—such had been the case with *The Interpretation of Dreams, Totem and Taboo,* and "The *Moses* of Michelangelo." But now his dissatisfaction was increased by awareness of the book's numerous faults—dilettantism, lack of method, unwarranted inferences—and fear that even friendly critics might notice them. And yet, despite the imperfections which he saw only too clearly, the book obsessed him, and continued to do so for years. At the end of 1934, he wrote to Arnold Zweig: "Don't say any more about the Moses book. The fact that this, probably my last creative effort, should have come to grief depresses me enough as it is. Not that I can shake him off. The man and what I wanted to make of him pursue me everywhere. But it would not do; the external dangers and my inner misgivings allow of no other solution. I think my memory of recent events is no longer reliable. The fact that I wrote at length to you in an earlier letter about Moses being an Egyptian is not the essential point, though it is the starting point. Nor is it any inner uncertainty on my part, for that is as good as settled, but the fact that I was obliged to construct so imposing a statue upon feet of clay, so that any fool could topple it."[23] Thus what obsessed Freud was not the historical problem of Jewish existence, as Moses himself, "the man and what I wanted to make of him."[24] Early in 1935 he confessed to Zweig: "Moses will not let go of my imagination. I picture myself reading it aloud to you when you come to Vienna, despite my defective speech. In an account of Tel el Amarna, which has not yet been fully excavated, I noticed a comment on a certain Prince Thotmes, of whom nothing further is known. If I were a millionaire, I would finance the continuation of the excavations. This Thotmes could be my Moses and I would be able to boast that I had guessed right."[25] And a month later: "As far as my productivity goes, it is like what happens in analysis. If a particular subject has been suppressed, nothing takes its place and the field of vision remains empty. So do I now remain fixated on the *Moses*, which has been laid aside and on which I can do no more. When may I read it to you?"[26] Yes, fixated he undoubtedly was, more than on any of his other books, but also tormented, distressed, so little at one with himself that he still spoke of his *Moses* as a project, even after half of it had been published. "Several years ago," he wrote to an anonymous correspondent, "I started asking myself how the Jews acquired their particular character, and following my usual custom, I went back to the earliest beginnings."[27] But he mentions neither the title of the book nor the fact that part of it had been published in a journal; indeed it was as though, just as his work was becoming a reality, he wished to thrust it back into the realm of vague possibility. The two published chapters brought him no peace; in the following year he worked on the third and noted that Moses was still tormenting him like a "ghost not laid."[28] Since he was by then approaching the end of his long career, it is hard to say whether he felt freed of his ghost toward the end or whether his preoccupation with Moses ended only with his life.

If Freud is to be taken at his word, what troubled him most was not his central thesis that Moses was an Egyptian, though of all his ideas it was by far the most adventurous. He took it as a certainty, and he assures us time and time again that the source of his greatest misgivings was elsewhere. But for one who had so brilliantly demonstrated the significance of *negation* in the grammar of neurosis[29] he seems to deny it too emphatically. The more he denies that his "Egyptian Moses" was the main cause of his difficulties, the more one inclines to think it was. And moreover none of the book's other themes can have appeared so scandalous in his eyes as to provoke his mysterious malaise. The theme of the leader murdered by the "mob" is common enough throughout history to seem plausible, even in the absence of conclusive evidence. And as for the far-reaching consequences of this murder committed at the dawn of our civilization, no regard for the religious sensibilities of any denomination whatever had deterred Freud from discussing them in *Totem and Taboo*. True, he may have felt uneasy to be considering the matter from the standpoint of the two great revealed religions rather than of religion in general as before, but it seems doubtful that his uneasiness would have sufficed to paralyze him. It was quite a different matter to deprive the founder of Jewish history of his identity while at the same time recognizing the reality of his person and the *unique* character of his founding. This was to rewrite the history of the Western world on the basis of a remote possibility; it was literally to turn the world upside down with a lever resting on an invisible fulcrum. It was to declare a whole people illegitimate, and worse, to tell the Jews that this ancient usurpation was the real reason why they were hated by the nations and unjustly persecuted.

This ruthless act of dispossession was far more likely than the supposed murder of Moses by the Jews and the related psychoanalytic theory of religion to provoke the inner panic reflected not only in Freud's letters, but also in the hesitant style and awkward form of the book itself. It is true that in 1934 he still had no way of foreseeing the Nazis' "final solution" to the problem,[30] but he knew enough about the ideology of the Third Reich to appreciate the full extent of the peril; and even if the situation of the Jews had been infinitely less tragic, the mere fact of "denaturalizing" their greatest prophet argued an aggressiveness of which he could hardly have been unaware. And indeed, he was so much aware of it that he justified himself in the very first lines of his essay, before the reader could even have known what he was about: "To deprive a people of the man whom they take pride in as the greatest of their sons is not a thing to be gladly or carelessly undertaken, least of all by someone who is himself one of them. But we cannot allow any such reflection to induce us to put the truth aside in favor of what are supposed to be national interests; and, moreover, the clarification of a set of facts may be expected to bring us a gain in knowledge."[31]

Obviously Freud took no pleasure in telling the Jews that

the greatest of their sons was not of their blood. Why then did he do so? Because, so he tells us, he had no right to conceal the truth, not even in order to spare his sorely tried people. (Interestingly the whole book contains not one reference to the recent events which, as Freud himself owned, had inspired it.) But since this truth that was so urgently in need of being divulged was a historical truth—the historic kernel beneath the slag of legend—one would assume that Freud had established it on the basis of facts, which others had disregarded or misunderstood, or of new evidence. But Freud makes no such claims; on almost every page he stresses the ungrateful nature of his subject, the uncertainty of his attempt at reconstruction, and the speculations to which he was driven by the necessity of filling in gaps. He had no proofs, but had to content himself with suggestions, inferences, and working hypotheses, and he foresaw the reproaches of his critics: "If no more certainty could be reached than this, why, it may be asked, have I brought this enquiry into public notice at all? I am sorry to say that even my justification for doing so cannot go beyond hints. For if one allows oneself to be carried away by the two arguments which I have put forward here, and if one sets out to take the hypothesis seriously that Moses was an aristocratic Egyptian, very interesting and far-reaching prospects are opened up. . . . Such weighty conclusions cannot, however, be founded on psychological probabilities alone. Even if one accepts the fact of Moses being an Egyptian as a first historic foothold, one would need to have at least a second firm fact in order to defend the wealth of emerging possibilities against the criticism of their being a product of the imagination and too remote from reality. Objective evidence of the period to which the life of Moses and with it the Exodus from Egypt are to be referred would perhaps have fulfilled this requirement. But this has not been obtainable, and it will therefore be better to leave unmentioned any further implications of the discovery that Moses was an Egyptian."[32] The end of this paragraph, which if taken at face value ought to have been the end of the book, postulates as a secure fact what was previously a mere combination of two shaky inferences: Moses was an Egyptian because his name could have been Egyptian; the Egyptian princess, represented as his foster-mother in the Bible story, was his mother. (This is inferred from a psychoanalytical decoding of his birth legend.) Nevertheless, Freud went on with the book, and the title of the second chapter ("If Moses was an Egyptian") reduces what had just been set up as an established truth to the level of an unproved hypothesis.

The argument is continued with a chain of "ifs" and "buts" which seem calculated more to obscure the possible objections than to refute them. One can only repeat the question that Freud himself asked at the outset: Why publish this book if no certainty was possible in the matter? Why offend and grieve the Jews, already overwhelmed with troubles, in the name of a "truth" that had no scientific foundation whatever and that ultimately reduced itself to a few "interesting" conjectures? And Freud's insistence on his "truth" seems all the more surprising when we consider that it was more of a hindrance than a help to the central thesis of the book. For Moses could perfectly well have been killed by the Jews without being an Egyptian; and moreover, if he was not a Jew he could be the father of the Hebrews only in a figurative sense, and his murder ceased to be the exemplary parricide by which Freud, resuming the theme of *Totem and Taboo*, explained the genesis of the most highly developed religions.

Then why rob the Jews of their prophet? Why should Freud, with a heavy heart, take a painful step that did not even advance the main thesis of the book? Did he merely wish to prove to himself that he could still create and still enhance his glory? That is most unlikely, and the book would hardly have lent itself to such a purpose, for he was profoundly dissatisfied with it to the very end. No, he had far more compelling reasons for his persistence, and he reveals them almost transparently in the subtitle "a historical novel," which he first gave the book: he did not want to die without writing the true novel of his life, and like every in-

153

spired novelist he was so utterly possessed by his fictitious world that he remained deaf to all reminders of reality.

His undertaking was no doubt favored by the fact that the historical novel had just come back into fashion. Thomas Mann, with whom he had been in constant touch—especially since 1930 when Mann had been instrumental in having the Goethe Prize awarded to Freud—was working on the first volume of his Joseph series; Mann's brother, Heinrich, Emil Ludwig, Stefan Zweig, and Lion Feuchtwanger all tried their hand at the genre, for the most part with considerable success.[33] Arnold Zweig, the "son" in whom Freud confided most readily at the time, was planning a documented novel on Nietzsche, halfway between history and psychoanalysis, and was asking his spiritual "father's" advice and help in the matter at the very time when Freud was communicating his own audacious views on the Exodus to Zweig. While hostile to Zweig's Nietzsche project,[34] Freud seems to have envied Mann his Joseph, to judge by the letter in which he apparently tried to convince Mann not only that Mann's biblical fable was incomplete but also that it was far more profound than he himself had suspected. Here Freud, consoling himself perhaps for not having been able, or not having dared, to follow his novelistic bent continued deep in his basement what Thomas Mann had constructed on the heights of his art. Thanks to a bit of interpretation which created a link between totally unrelated symbolic figures—the Joseph of the Bible, famed for his art of interpreting dreams, and Bonaparte, the invincible conqueror—Freud resumed the novelistic confession begun forty years before between the lines of the Traumdeutung. For as an interpreter of dreams Joseph was in a sense Freud's double and the true guiding spirit of the Traumdeutung, so that Freud was actually speaking of himself in his subtle analysis of an extraordinary destiny—of himself and the irresistible passion that still impelled him to rewrite his life.

Napoleon had an elder brother named Joseph, who played the part of Destiny itself in his adventurous existence. In a highly traditional Corsican family, in which the "privilege of the eldest was guarded with a particularly sacred awe . . . the elder brother is the natural rival; the younger one feels for him an elemental, unfathomably deep hostility," which with the years changes to hatred and thoughts of murder. "To eliminate Joseph, to take his place, to become Joseph himself, must have been Napoleon's strongest emotion as a small child." But excessive infantile impulses tend to turn into their opposite, so that the most hated becomes the most loved later on. After having detested Joseph, Napoleon loved him more than anyone in the world and "could hardly find a fault in this worthless, unreliable young man." However, "the early aggression released was only waiting to be transferred to other objects. Hundreds of thousands of unknown individuals had to atone for the fact that this little tyrant had spared his first enemy." It was Joseph and none other who inspired his passion for Josephine; and he again, concealed behind profound political designs, who decided him to undertake his famous Egyptian campaign. "Where else could one go but Egypt if one were Joseph and wanted to loom large in the brother's eyes? . . . It was this campaign, by the way, that marked the beginning of Egypt's rediscovery. The intention which drove Napoleon to Egypt was to be realized in his later life in Europe. He took care of his brothers by making them kings and princes. The good-for-nothing Jerome was perhaps his Benjamin. But then he forsook his myth; he allowed himself to be swayed by practical considerations, to repudiate his beloved Josephine. With this act his decline began."[35] Of course Freud, the modern Joseph, was not able to give real thrones to the members of his family; in his own way, however, he took the same path as the conqueror, for he too managed to bend history to the grandiose designs of his "family novel." And in this he was even more successful than Napoleon, the younger brother, for thus far he had remained faithful to his mythology.

The desire to refashion his biography, which as we have seen figures prominently in his dreams as recorded in the *Traumdeutung*, led Freud to take a passionate interest not only in everything connected with the mystery of birth and origins, but also in shadowy individuals whose established identity could in any way be questioned. In this same period, along with his continued obsession with Moses, his longtime interest in the identity of Shakespeare took on a new and almost incredible intensity.[36] Shakespeare held a place equal to Goethe's in Freud's pantheon, but by a strange quirk, he absolutely refused to consider the possibility that Shakespeare might simply have been himself, a commoner of English extraction. The problem, which has long been a subject of learned controversy, had tormented him for years. As a young man, after hearing his teacher Meynert defend the Baconian theory, he wrote to Martha: "If that were so, then Bacon would have been the most powerful brain the world has ever produced, whereas it seems to me that there is more need to share Shakespeare's achievement among several rivals than to burden another important man with it."[37] A few years before the First World War he urged Ernest Jones "to make a thorough study of the methods of interpretation employed by the Baconians, contrasting them with psychoanalytic methods."[38] Though Jones, as we can well imagine, showed no great eagerness to undertake this task, Freud kept prodding him. "But was Shakespeare really an Englishman," he wrote, "and was his name what it appeared to be, compared with Brakespeare and so on? He was taken with a suggestion by an Italian, Gentilli, that it was simply a corruption of Jacques Pierre; and indeed Shakespeare's features appeared more Latin than English. That was in the days when physical anthropologists tended to confound nations with primitive races and to make far-reaching inferences from skull measurements."[39]

This confusion of nation with race, which Jones rightly attributes to a tendency of the times, goes hand in hand with confusion of race and language, and of this Freud's "Egyptian Moses" is a perfect example. Moses was an Egyptian because his name, to judge by its etymology, may have been Egyptian, and his race derived automatically from his nationality. To Freud all this was self-evident, and necessarily so, for without this prejudice characteristic of the anthropology of the day, his novel would have lost all semblance of a foundation in reality.

One might have expected his interest in the Shakespeare problem to wane with time, but in point of fact the older he grew the more it fascinated him. In 1920, after reading a book by one Thomas Looney, who identified Shakespeare with Edward de Vere, seventeenth Earl of Oxford, he gradually came to believe that he held the key to the enigma and tried to win over his friends, to whom he imputed the same passion for the subject. Obviously Looney's theory appealed to Freud because it purged Shakespeare's biography of the two elements that Freud was most eager to eliminate: his English extraction and above all his status as a commoner, which conflicted with the tendencies of his own "family novel" and his profound need of aristocratic origins. The passion with which he defended this "fantasy" of a second-rate author was a source of astonishment to his friends. On May 5, 1926, his seventieth birthday, he spent the evening with Jones, Ferenczi, and Eitingon. "He expounded the de Vere theory to us at length," Jones writes. "I remember my astonishment at the enthusiasm he could display on the subject at two in the morning."[40] In 1930 he even managed to work the seventeenth Earl of Oxford into his message of thanks to the jury which had just awarded him the Goethe Prize.[41] In 1935 he added the following note to the passage in his autobiographical study connecting the writing of Hamlet with the death of Shakespeare's father: "This is a construction which I should like explicitly to withdraw. I no longer believe that William Shakespeare the actor from Stratford was the author of the works which have so long been attributed to him. Since the publication of Looney's volume 'Shakespeare Identified,' I am almost convinced that in fact Edward de Vere, Earl of Oxford, is concealed behind this pseudonym."[42] And in the year of his death he reiterates this conviction in 'An Outline of Psychoanalysis,' as though determined to the very end to clear Shakespeare of the original taint—lowly birth—which only his own dreams of grandeur had been able to expunge in himself.

The novel which Freud in his secret imagination built up on Shakespeare throws a bright light on the astonishing work he was doing in his *Moses* at the same time and for the same quite unobjective reasons. In both cases he deprived a people of its greatest genius, but the example of Shakespeare shows that he did so for compelling unconscious reasons, and not at all out of resentment or animosity. England was his favorite European country; for years he dreamed of England as the country where he would like best to take refuge if he were ever obliged to leave Vienna. Indeed it was there that he found a haven in 1938, and it was the enthusiastic welcome of the London crowd which first convinced him that he was really famous.[43] No one could possibly believe that he wished with his myth of Shakespeare's birth to injure the poet's native land, and still less that he wished to favor France, a country to which for several reasons he was not greatly drawn. (His stay in Paris at the time of his greatest poverty had not left him with very pleasant memories, and he was disheartened by the incomprehension of French scientific circles, which in the main continued to reject him.) Of course the case of the poet did not coincide exactly with that of the prophet; high as Freud placed Shakespeare in his spiritual hierarchy, he remained a foreigner; Moses, on the other hand, was a part of his own being, and he could not deface his image without doing himself a grave injury. But be that as it may, Freud's two biographical fictions had this in common: they owed nothing to outward circumstances. Just as Freud supported Looney's extravagant thesis on Shakespeare for reasons that had nothing to do with love or hatred for one country or another, so his Moses did not result directly, or primarily, or consciously from the hatred of the Jews that some critics have read between the lines of his book. It is only the last episode in the novel of origins on which Freud worked all his life and which toward the end took on the force of truth.

Nothing he said or did in this period indicates a change in

his attitude toward his people; at the most he had grown more impatient with anything that he interpreted as Jewish baseness or cowardice. This had always been a sore point with him—ever since his father had told him about picking up his cap out of the mud—and now in the agitated world of the thirties there was plenty to shock his sensibilities. At such times anecdotes heavily seasoned with black humor are even more popular than usual among the Jews and one day Freud mistook such an anecdote for an actual news item. The story was that the Jews of Berlin had paraded through the streets carrying banners with the device: "Throw us out!" Believing this had really happened, Freud immediately gave vent to his indignation in a letter to Arnold Zweig. According to Jones, who mentions the letter, but unfortunately does not quote it, Freud went so far as to say that such undignified behavior was typical of the Jewish character and his only consolation was that these people were half German.[44] On the whole, however, such reactions of wounded love and pride are less frequent in his correspondence than frank expressions of loyalty. In the letter of 1936, speaking of David Eder, the only psychoanalyst of the first generation to have been a militant Zionist, Freud is far from denigrating the Jewish character and speaks with admiration of the "mysterious thing that makes the Jew." And in a letter written in that same year to Arnold Zweig, who complained of being unable to adapt himself to Palestine, Freud states his views on the national homeland if not on Zionism: "Your letter moved me very much. It is not the first time I have heard of the difficulties the cultured man finds in adapting himself to Palestine. History has never given the Jewish people cause to develop their faculty for creating a state or a society. And of course they take with them into their new abode all the shortcomings and vices of the culture of the country they leave behind them. You feel ill at ease, but I did not know you found isolation so hard to bear. Firmly based in your profession as artist as you are, you ought to be able to be alone for a while. In Palestine at any rate you have your personal safety and your human rights.

And where would you think of going? You would find America, I would say from all my impressions, far more unbearable. Everywhere else you would be a scarcely tolerated alien . . . I really think that for the moment you should remain where you are."[45] Here, along with the obvious affection we discern a mild reproach, but it is not addressed to the Jew in Zweig. On the contrary, if he complained about life in Palestine it was because he was still too German, too deeply marked by the shortcomings and vices of the culture he had left behind. In a letter of the same period, he wrote: "It is typically Jewish not to renounce anything and to replace what has been lost."[46] And he showed perfect loyalty to his people when on March 13, 1938, shortly before going into exile, he informed Zweig that he had decided to walk in the footsteps of his great Jewish ancestors and despite his advanced years to rebuild his School in a new Jabneh.

It is not so very surprising that Freud, assailed at the age of eighty-two by the insoluble problems which for over a century had periodically shaken Western Jewry—assimilation, traditionalism, apostasy, Zionism, emigration—should have presented a rather hazy picture of his opinions, in which it is not always easy to tell what he really meant. Buffeted from one extreme to the other by news reports that could not always be verified; horrified by events which for all his pessimism he had never thought possible; rendered more emotionally vulnerable than ever before by old age and illness—Freud made quite a few questionable statements in those days. But whatever one may think of the fluctuations in his thinking, the fact remains that his *Moses* did not spring primarily from the contradictory emotions aroused in him by the tragic events of the day, but was rooted in his most remote past, in his need to reconsider the facts of his birth, to change them at least in his imagination and so become master of his fate.

If Freud had stuck to his original idea of a "historical novel," he might have avoided a good deal of regretful or acrimonious criticism. No one would have contested his Balzacian right to "compete with the registry office," that is, to create whatever genealogies he saw fit. He would have written a kind of historical fiction claiming only to communicate a certain amount of *psychic* truth as any novel is entitled to do. But once he abandoned his projected novel for a scientific work, he staked his good name as a scientist on a dubious undertaking, which instead of serving science and history, exploited them unscrupulously. Theology was of course the first discipline to take offense, but others—philology, archaeology, epigraphy, anthropology, and even genetics—might also have found fault with his way of handling their methods and findings. From Freud's point of view, which was of course that of an agnostic scientist, their objections would have been more cogent than those of the theologians, for they professed the same principles as he did and the same respect for intellectual integrity. Yet for various reasons, among them no doubt the publication date (1939), most of the specialists best equipped to answer Freud refrained from doing so. As a result, the book was reviewed almost exclusively by the most prejudiced of critics, Christian theologians and orthodox Jews.

Yet as a work on monotheism based on interpretation of the Scriptures, the *Moses* invited the criticism of a school of exegesis whose views would no doubt have appealed to Freud if he had been more familiar with them. The "liberal" or "independent" exegetes had discarded the orthodox view that sacred texts cannot be studied in the same way as profane texts; they held that a sacred text may sometimes demand greater care because of its greater antiquity, but that on the whole the interpretation of the two kinds of text is subject to the same laws and calls for the same exacting method. In both cases the student must make the fullest use of all related disciplines—philology, epigraphy, archaeology, religious, political and social history—in appraising his documents and seeking to determine their age, state of preservation, degree of authenticity, etc. The content of a sacred text can be established with some degree of certainty only after elimination of all the interpolations by scribes or scholiasts, which in the course of time have come to be regarded as integral parts of the texts. But once this work of sifting has been done, it is often possible to reconstitute a plausible chain of events.

On the strength of such investigations the liberal exegetes contend that the text of the Bible as a whole, especially of the historical books, is neither as authentic as the orthodox would have it, nor as spurious as the skeptics claim. For though the Pentateuch, for example, was not and could not have been written by Moses himself (if only because it records his death), it does not follow that the whole of it is made up of legend, folklore, or the deliberately tendentious inventions of priests and scribes, as agnostic amateurs tend to believe. What makes these books so difficult to interpret is not deliberate or unconscious falsification, which would make the whole story of the Exodus a plain forgery, but the peculiar, and to modern eyes illogical, way in which the ancient chroniclers, both sacred and profane, handled the texts on which their narratives are based. Working with manuscripts originating in different traditions, they made no attempt to collate them and derive a coherent narrative, but merely copied everything verbatim in no discernible order. In this the Pentateuch is no exception, for, to quote Adolphe Lods: "All the historical books of the Old Testament—and they make up almost half of it—are compilations of earlier books which the editors combined by reproducing them almost textually."[47] This accounts for the doublets, the repetitions, the incoherences and anachronisms which adulterate the authentic tradition; it accounts for the traps that the exegete must guard against; and it explains why the person and story of Moses as recorded in the Bible are confused and contradictory.

Of course Freud read a number of specialized works for *Moses*—he cites Ed. Meyer, Auerbach, Hugo Gressmann, Ernst Sellin—but he paid little attention to questions of method, for he was chiefly interested in findings that squared with his own ideas. The arbitrariness of his procedure did not escape him, but he thought nothing of it, for convinced as he was that the entire text of the Pentateuch was a deliberate forgery, he held that no other writer could claim to be closer to the truth. "I am very well aware," he wrote in a footnote, "that in dealing so autocratically and arbitrarily with biblical tradition—bringing it up to confirm my views when it suits me and unhesitatingly rejecting it when it contradicts me—I am exposing myself to serious methodological criticism and weakening the force of my arguments. *But this is the only way in which one can treat material of which one knows that its trustworthiness has been severely impaired by the distorting influence of tendentious purposes.* It is to be hoped that I shall find some degree of justification later on, when I come upon the track of these secret motives. Certainty is in any case unattainable and moreover it may be said that every other writer on the subject has adopted the same procedure."[48]

By a paradox of which Freud was assuredly unaware, this total skepticism concerning the historical content of the biblical texts is the one point in which Freud's view concurs with that of the orthodox exegetes. For though Freud knew that the Pentateuch was made up of strands of diverse origin, though he knew of the two narrators, "J" and "E," the "Jahvist" and the "Elohist," and was aware of the anachronisms that indicate the heterogeneous character of the compilation, he disregarded this knowledge when it came to constructing his theory, and like the orthodox theologians persisted in confusing the time when the events of the Exodus took place with the very much more recent period when they were committed to writing. While for the liberal exegete attempting to extricate Moses from the mists of legend it is obvious that "if we wish to confine ourselves to the realm of sure facts the most we can do is reconstitute those parts of his work whose consequences were still felt at the time in which our first reliable documents came into being," for Freud it was possible to speak of the prophet as though we had direct evidence of his life. Forgetting that our image of Moses is as vague and incomplete as "our image of Jesus, for example, would be, if we were obliged to re-construct it on the basis of a handful of facts concerning the beliefs and practices of the Christians of the third or fourth centuries,"[49] he proceeds as though he had concrete and di-rect knowledge of the lawgiver, his contemporaries, and the events of their lives. And while elsewhere he shows himself to be a convinced evolutionist, here he implicitly negates the very principle of evolution by thinking away the eight hundred-odd years required for the biblical image to take form. True, the anachronism serves his purpose: it provides him with the *immediate* hero without which his attempt at psychological analysis would lose all semblance of justifica-tion.

Unfortunately, liberal Bible criticism shows that it is im-possible to know Moses as an individual; we can only gain a vague knowledge of him "through the parts of his work, whose consequences were still felt at the time in which our first reliable documents came into being"; in other words, we are curtained off from him by several centuries of thought and culture. Under these conditions Moses, the human individual, cannot possibly be subjected to psycho-logical analysis; at the very most one might analyze the *edi-tors,* who successively compiled the ancient chronicles relat-ing his life, for Moses has no existence except in their narratives; he is made in the image of their ethical, social, and spiritual needs, and apart from a few faintly intimated character traits reflects only the psychology of the intel-lectual elite of various epochs. Freud, needless to say, was not at all interested in the chroniclers of the eighth or sixth century B.C., who to all intents and purposes had provided him with his subject. What interested him was the "original" man and people whose thoughts and actions of course had to be consonant with his own vision. Thus he rewrote the life of Moses as though deliberately forgetting the dense layer of time which must obscure the prophet's true face forever. He also rewrote the prophet's death so as to make it a tragedy, and in this, sacrilegious as it may seem, he followed directly in the footsteps not of the modern critics but of the old storytellers of the Talmud, merely adding a legend of his own fabrication to all those that the Jews, moved by fervent piety and also perhaps by an unconscious desire to free themselves from a crushing spiritual burden, have from time immemorial woven around the person of the unparalleled hero in whom their entire destiny is epitomized.[50]

We are now in a position to trace the course of Freud's "family novel" through the two essential works in which it is recorded—the *Traumdeutung*, in which the fantasies of Freud's nights are presented in their constant relation to the realities of his days and then subjected to an analysis which, though incompletely published, is carried on with perfect impartiality, as though at a distance from the dreamer; and *Moses and Monotheism*, where, in the impersonal form of a summary of psychoanalytical theory as applied to the origins of civilization,[51] the novel takes its leave of history and the real world of necessity and pursues its own aims. This extraordinary turn in the family myth is adequately explained by the author's age; at forty, Freud had disavowed his father for reasons that were still eminently those of life; at eighty he again disavowed him, but now precisely because he had nothing to look forward to but the forbidding prospect of mental decline and death. A dreamer but still a realist as long as he was actively struggling to rise to a leading position "on the other side," now, with the struggle far behind him and nothing ahead but the end of all existence he abandoned himself once more to the utter unreality of a dream. The maturing adult of the *Traumdeutung* tried to liberate himself in dreams from his Jewish father—a mediocrity who did nothing to overcome the confinement of his existence within the intolerable limits of inferior birth. Clearly the old man of the *Moses* was in an entirely different situation. Numbered among the most illustrious men of his time, he had no further interest in titles or ranks. It was precisely because he took his dreams seriously that he had been able to fulfill his wildest ambitions step by step, but for all his success he was still obsessed by the problem of origins, or more precisely, he could not rest before proposing one more solution in an attempt to break the chain of the generations and so free himself forever from all the fathers, parents, and ancestors who conspired to remind him of man's intolerable limitations.

Shortly before his death, Freud was seized with a last stirring of revolt against the inexorable fatality of filiation, which so narrowly limits every man by burdening him with an origin, a race, and a name. Frightened by his increasingly marked resemblance to Jakob Freud, he fought with all his strength against this "return of the repressed" which, beginning in middle life, foreshadows the slow extinction of a man's individuality. For human individuality is short-lived; it is late to develop in the child, who cannot become an individual without rebelling against his dependence toward his parents and against his need to identify with their revered image. Emerging from his struggle to free himself from the domination of his forebears, the adult is convinced that he has finally become a separate individual, unique in character and disposition; but with old age, the most individual of individuals becomes again the replica of his parents. "In his old age," we read in *Moses and Monotheism*, "even the great Goethe, who in his years of storm and stress had undoubtedly looked down upon his unbending and pedantic father, developed traits that had formed part of his father's character."[52] Here Freud, who had always identified himself with Goethe, was undoubtedly alluding to the painful loss of individuality that he himself was experiencing: at the approach of death, he was becoming more and more like Jakob, threatened by a "return of the repressed" that was gradually destroying his personality. It is no accident that he devotes a whole chapter of his book to this second identification with the father, the terrible outcome of which is only too easily foreseeable; in writing it he wished no doubt to establish his mastery, at least in spirit, over the inevitable process of his own dissolution. Indeed, he may well have been moved to write the story of Moses and his people primarily by a desire to suspend for some little time the dreaded moment of return—"return of the repressed" and eternal and inevitable return to the bosom of his forefathers. For the regressive movement which makes an old man over in the image of his father takes the exact opposite direction from that which informs the "family novel"; it destroys the individual by once more subjecting him to the laws of biology, to precisely what the child "novelist" does his best to deny by designing an autobiography out of the whole cloth. Seen in this light, Freud's last novel becomes the brilliant expedient of a mind confronted by necessity. As a fiction inspired by a revolutionary rejection of things as they are, and above all by an intransigent refusal of blood ties, it was the son's last protest and bulwark against the inevitable return of the fathers.

And so, in order not to die, Freud declared in the book that may be regarded as his authentic testament, that he was not Solomon son of Jakob, nor yet Sigmund the turncoat son, whose very name gave promise of the highest destinies, that he was no more a Jew than Moses had been, although the Jewish people had been born of this foreign leader and guide. But just as Moses had broken with his native Egypt and its rulers, who persecuted him for his advanced ideas, so Freud severed all inner ties with the Germany of his time, and not only with the Germany of the Nazis but with everything within him that was still German. So that when it came time for him to leave the stage where he had filled his role so valiantly, he could say that he was neither a Jew, nor a German, nor anything that still bore a name; for he wished to be the son not of any man or country, but like the murdered prophet only of his life work.

NOTES

I. OEDIPUS-FREUD, SON OF JAKOB

[1] David Bakan in his *Sigmund Freud and the Jewish Mystical Tradition* (Princeton, 1958), attempts to fill this gap, but unsuccessfully, because in identifying from the start the "Jewish spirit" that inspires Freud with the spirit of the Cabala, Bakan eludes the thorniest question, namely: By what mysterious channels could the cabalistic doctrine, or any other traditional dogma, have been transmitted to an unbelieving Jew, to an "extreme rationalist" as he himself put it, who, as we know, was hostile by temperament to mysticism of any kind and who moreover was without the slightest trace of an education in this special field? (The author cannot claim to have answered this question by stressing the birthplace of Freud's mother or by telling us that Freud may have read Abulafia or conceivably been influenced in this direction by Wilhelm Fliess, who had allegedly been initiated by some unnamed master. No parallel can be drawn between Freudian theory and any mystical tradition whatsoever unless we ignore everything Freud thought and said on the subject of such parallels. Quite a few authors make the same mistake. The moment they take up questions of philosophy, *Weltanschauung*, or religion, they tend to disregard the opinions which Freud stated most clearly and to which he was most attached, as though the mere fact that he was the first to throw light on the hidden motivations of our opinions justified them in ignoring his personal convictions. I shall have more to say on this confusion between Freud's express opinions, which, like any other element of his biography, have their historic existence, and the unconscious motives

that certain writers, bent on proving that he was lacking in self-knowledge, feel justified in imputing to him.

2 This is also the thesis of Heinrich Graetz, who, for example, has the following to say of Spinoza: "Once again the Jewish race had given birth to a profound thinker who was radically to cure the human mind of its ingrained errors and give it a new direction whereby to achieve a better understanding of the relations between heaven and earth and mind and body" (*Volkstümliche Geschichte der Juden*, Vienna and Berlin, 1888, 3 vols., Vol. III, p. 375). Here Spinoza's mission is described in terms that apply word for word to Freud. "The Jewish race once more brought a deep thinker into the world, one who was radically to heal the human mind of its rooted perversities and errors, and to prescribe a new direction for it, that it might better comprehend the connection between heaven and earth, between mind and matter." H. Graetz, *History of the Jews*, Vol. V (Philadelphia, 1895), p. 86.

3 Freud, "Address to the Society of B'nai B'rith," SE XX, p. 274. Freud puts forward a similar opinion in his homage to Josef Popper, known as the Lynx, who thanks to his *moral courage* almost discovered the theory of dreams before him. See "Josef Popper-Lynkeus and the Theory of Dreams," SE XIX, pp. 261ff.

4 Freud, "An Autobiographical Study," SE XX, p. 9.

5 *Freud/Pfister Letters*, p. 63.

6 *Freud/Abraham Letters*, p. 34. [Translation slightly modified.]

7 Ibid., p. 46.

8 Ibid., p. 36.

9 Here there is no need to say whether Freud was right or wrong. The numerous "Jewish" apostasies that occurred before and after 1908 (Adler, Rank, Reich, to cite only the best-known names) would seem to discredit this theory, but he may well have thought the Christian "apostasies" more

gravely regressive, since for the most part they tended to re-store the old manner of thinking (by a return to religion or to a more or less modernized mysticism). Still, whether we regard this notion as justified or as singularly one-sided, which in a sense it is, it belongs to the body of thoughts and feelings by which Freud manifests his consciousness of being a Jew, and to that extent it has its truth.

[10] Freud's letters have not all been published. In particular, his correspondence with Sandor Ferenczi is unavailable but is, I believe, in process of publication. As for the published letters—those to Oskar Pfister, Karl Abraham, Lou Andreas-Salomé, and Arnold Zweig—the editing is not beyond reproach. Whole letters have been omitted, others have been mutilated in varying degree, and for the most part the dele-tions made by the literary editor, Ernst L. Freud, are in-dicated unclearly or not at all. The gaps in this censored correspondence limit its value, and in making use of it one must bear in mind that passages which might clarify, confirm, or in certain cases even correct Freud's thought are lacking.

[11] The journal *Imago* contains numerous papers of this kind. By and large their authors present their findings more as curiosities than as reliable facts on which general conclusions can be based. Cf. also A. A. Roback, *Freudiana* (Cambridge, Massachusetts, 1957), which contains unpublished letters by Freud.

[12] Letter to Franz Werfel, probably not mailed. Cf. the let-ters to Max Brod and Franz Werfel of December 1922, in *Briefe 1902–1924*, ed. Max Brod (New York, Schocken, 1958), pp. 423ff. These two letters to Werfel were not mailed, but from the mere fact that Kafka kept them we may conclude that they are an accurate expression of his thought.

[13] Not to mention the authors who take a long leap through the centuries that carries them straight back to the Bible. Manes Sperber for example has suggested that psycho-analysis is "the Old Testament expressed in terms of psy-

chology" (*Le Talon d'Achille*, Paris, 1957, p. 172). Kafka would probably not have understood this idea, nor Freud either for that matter.

[14] Karl Kraus, *Literatur, oder Man wird doch da sehn. Eine magische Operette*, Vienna, 1921.

[15] Kafka, *Briefe 1902–1924* (New York, Schocken Books, 1958), p. 337.

[16] "Letter to His Father," in *Dearest Father: Stories and Other Writings*, tr. Ernest Kaiser and Eithne Wilkins (New York, Schocken, 1954), pp. 138ff.

[17] In the same letter, Kafka refers to the mental instability of his Jewish fellow students at the German Gymnasium in Prague, quite a few of whom, he tells us, committed suicide before completing their studies.

[18] The classical opposition between Hellenism and Judaism inspired Freud with intense remorse, as though his love of Greece had been a mark of apostasy. Cf. the letter he wrote to Romain Rolland on this subject at the age of eighty: "A Disturbance of Memory on the Acropolis," SE XXII, p. 239ff. I shall have more to say of it later on.

II. THE TWO CULTURES

[1] Ludwig Börne, Letter to Jeannette Wohl, Paris, February 7, 1832, quoted in *Juden und Judentum in deutschen Briefen aus drei Jahrhunderten* (Vienna, 1935), p. 243.

[2] Franz Kafka, *The Castle* (New York, 1969), p. 32. This novel, which has been greatly misunderstood, centers entirely on this question of resemblances which, for the outsider, partakes of magic. K. shows himself to be a foreigner in two ways: by his desire to resemble Gerstäcker and Lasemann, and by his inability to distinguish between the inhabitants of the Village; to his eyes all the peasants look the same; his assistants seem to him so much alike that he treats them as one man and calls them both Arthur; he is also una-

ble to distinguish them from his messenger and that is what dooms him. This magic, which denatures the *vision* of all the characters and seriously affects their relations with each other, is one of the many reasons why *The Castle* cannot be transposed into a play or film.

[3] On this aspect of the situation see Isaiah Berlin, *Trois essais sur la condition juive* (Paris, 1973), pp. 164ff.

[4] *Freud/A. Zweig Letters*, p. 40: ". . . and we hail from there [Palestine] (though one of us considers himself a German as well; the other does not) . . ."

[5] Letter of February 2, 1886, to Martha Bernays, *Letters*, p. 203. "Only toward the end I embarked on a political discussion with Gilles de la Tourette, during which of course he predicted the most ferocious war with Germany. I promptly explained that I am a Jew, adhering neither to Germany nor Austria. But such conversations are always very embarrassing to me, for I feel stirring within me something German which I long ago decided to suppress." A few months before, he had written to the same Martha (ibid., p. 188): "As you realize, my heart is German provincial," proving that he had not been very successful in suppressing the "something German" in him.

[6] Concerning Freud's attitude during the first years of World War I, see *Freud/Abraham Letters*.

[7] Since psychoanalysis came into being shortly after Jakob Freud's death, Freud's first students did not know the man whom destiny had so oddly chosen to be the instrumentality of a new truth. Some, however, were well acquainted with Amalia Freud, his mother, whose mythical role of "Oedipean mother" must not lead us to forget the flesh-and-blood woman. According to the recollections of Theodor Reik, she had retained the language, the manners, and probably the beliefs of her native environment. She spoke broken German well seasoned with Yiddish. (Cf. E. Freeman, *Conversations with Theodor Reik*, Prentice Hall, 1971.)

[8] *The Interpretation of Dreams*, SE IV, p. 197.

[9] Letter of February 20, 1930, to A. A. Roback. *Letters,* p. 395. Cf. also A. A. Roback, *Freudiana,* pp. 230, 231. Actually Freud did not write "lack in my education," but *"dieses Stück meiner Unbildung,"* "this piece of my ignorance," and the nuance is significant in view of the part played in Freud's inner life by his father's ignorance of Western civilization. Here he is the ignorant one, for he does not know Hebrew, in which his father was well versed.

[10] See Jones I, pp. 160, 163, 167, 223. Cf. also Marthe Robert, *La Révolution psychoanalytique,* Vol. I, pp. 125 and 126.

[11] Cf. Roback, who reproduces and analyzes the flyleaf of the Bible with Jakob Freud's dedication.

[12] See Roback, pp. 95, 96.

[13] Jones I, p. 19, translation slightly amended. Jakob does not address his son as Solomon in Jones's version. A more literal translation may be found in Roback, p. 92.

[14] *The Interpretation of Dreams,* SE IV, p. 173.

[15] "A Disturbance of Memory on the Acropolis," SE XXII, pp. 246ff. Cf. above Chapter I, Note 18. On this trip in 1904 Freud was accompanied by his brother Alexander, who was ten years his junior, as was Romain Rolland, to whom Freud was writing to congratulate him on his seventieth birthday.

[16] In this Freud was by no means alone. Jones (I, p. 192) quotes Ernst Freud as saying that his grandfather Jakob was a great admirer of Bismarck. Many German Jews felt the same way regardless of their degree of assimilation.

[17] *Juden und Judentum,* p. 393. Letter of Rathenau to the lawyer Apfel, November 16, 1918.

[18] *Juden und Judentum,* p. 378. Letter of Georg Brandes to Henri Nathanson, June 11, 1903.

[19] *The Interpretation of Dreams,* the *"Non-vixit* Dream." Discus. Avon ed. 1965, pp. 456ff.

[20] "One day a young man who had passed through a technical training college introduced himself with a manuscript which showed very unusual comprehension. We persuaded

him to go through the *Gymnasium* [secondary school] and the University and devote himself to the nonmedical side of psychoanalysis." *On the History of the Psychoanalytic Movement*, SE XIV, p. 25. Freud does not tell us that he helped to support Rank for years and that it was entirely thanks to him that Rank was enabled to study and to become enormously learned in the space of a few years. Theodor Reik was in the same situation; he remembers that Freud gave him money every month throughout his period of study and even for a long time after his marriage. Lou Andreas-Salomé might also have testified to his unstinting generosity.

[21] Letter to Stefan Zweig, February 7, 1931. *Letters*, pp. 402ff.

[22] This is especially true of *Group Psychology and the Analysis of the Ego*, but the same attitude may be found elsewhere, in particular, in *Totem and Taboo* and *Moses and Monotheism*.

[23] *Letters*, p. 6.

[24] Cf. the analysis of the "My friend R. was my uncle" dream in *The Interpretation of Dreams*, SE IV, pp. 137ff., in which the memory of the marvelous prophecies made to Freud in his childhood was associated with his memory of Jewish cabinet ministers, the "middle class ministry," and the high hopes cherished by every "industrious little Jew" at the time.

[25] In 1873 Georg von Schönerer, a left-wing anti-Semite, the first politician to combine racism with violent anticapitalism, was elected to the Austrian Reichsrat. On Schönerer and Adolf Stöcker, the pioneer of German political anti-Semitism, see Peter G. J. Pulzer, *The Rise of Political Anti-Semitism in Germany and Austria* (New York, 1964).

[26] On the liberalism of the secondary schools in Austro-Hungary we have the testimony of Theodor Herzl in an autobiographical note published by the *Jewish Chronicle*, January 14, 1898, and quoted by Nicolas Baudy in *Les Grandes questions juives* (Éditions Planète, 1968), p. 138.

[27] "Ein Duktus des Gehirns." Letter from Gustav Landauer to the philologist Fritz Mauthner, November 20, 1913, in *Juden und Judentum*, p. 382. In this letter Gustav Landauer, who some years later was to take part in the German revolution and play a leading role in the Munich "Soviet Republic," states a position so close to Freud's that it seems worth quoting: "I suggest that we put an end to our argument about the Jews . . . The essential is not that you should characterize what is distinctive in the Jewish makeup as 'nothing but a convolution of the brain'; the essential is that in terming this convolution Jewish you are speaking not only of a trait peculiar to you as an individual, but of something you have in common with a great many. If I am asked what value I attach to this community born of a common history, logic is no help to me. In the present period, I cannot find enough communities reaching back thousands of years to make me forgo a single one, and besides I have no reason to. A community that can be recognized by a 'convolution of the brain,' as you put it, implies a considerable reality. Thus we have a feeling coexisting with a reality: logic cannot take it away from me, and why should it want to?"

[28] Wise man, title of the head of the local Sephardic community.

[29] Fast Day in memory of the destruction of the Temple in Jerusalem (586 B.C.).

[30] *Letters,* p. 18ff. [Translation slightly modified.]

[31] Not only here, but wherever he touches on the subject in his work. He ignores the Cabala and takes an interest only in the legalist, rationalist current of Judaism, in which alone he found "affinities of intellectual temperament." The Freudian theory of religion, according to which religious beliefs and practices have their source in the same mechanisms as obsessional neurosis, so that neurosis and religion are closely related, squares perfectly with ritualist Judaism, but not nearly as well with the religions in which dogma and theological speculation, are far more important than ritual. Generally

speaking, Freud did not carry his analysis of religious states very far; they are all lumped together (from 1914 on) and explained by the fundamental narcissism of the psyche.

[82] Jones makes very little of Freud's relation to Judaism and of its importance for his work. Theodor Reik (see Chapter II, Note 7) remarks first that Jones had no understanding of things Jewish, which seems likely, and secondly that this curious omission might well connote a bit of repressed anti-Semitism, an assertion which of course cannot be proved. Be that as it may, it seems plausible to suppose that Jones, writing as a conscientious humanist and a naïve believer in the universality of ideas, thought it preferable to concentrate on what seemed universal in Freud and to minimize his Jewishness, as though it had been a purely accidental circumstance, interesting as a picturesque bit of biography, but of no great importance for the development of Freudian psychology. Wishing to represent his master as a universal thinker—which indeed he was, but precisely because he lived an individual destiny in the most individual way, and not by virtue of some transcendent privilege—Jones neglected to look into the relation between the particular and the general in this special instance, the particular being Freud in his position on the fringe of his adoptive society, and the general being the Freudian theory of the human psyche. From the start he represents Freud as a scientific genius battling the intellectual philistines. By taking this cliché (which, to be sure, becomes a truth later in Freud's career) as his starting point, Jones obscures Freud's basic originality and deprives his hero of a good part of his reality.

[83] Freud was the victim of an incident of this kind on a train that was taking him to Leipzig. He was so much upset that he reported it immediately in a letter to Martha: "You know how I am always longing for fresh air and always anxious to open windows, above all in trains. So I opened a window and stuck my head out to get a breath of air. Whereupon there were shouts to shut it . . . I declared my willingness to close the window provided another, opposite, were opened;

it was the only opened window in the whole long carriage. While the discussion went on and the man said he was prepared to open the ventilation slit instead of the window, there came a shout from the background: 'He's a dirty Jew!' —And with this the whole situation took on a different color. . . . Even a year ago I would have been speechless with agitation, but now I am different. I was not in the least frightened of that mob. I asked the one to keep to himself his empty phrases that impressed me not at all, and the other to step up and take what was coming to him. I was quite prepared to kill him, but he did not step up . . ." Letter of December 16, 1883. *Letters*, p. 78. [Translation slightly modified.]

[84] Letter of January 6, 1885. *Letters*, p. 131.

[85] Letter of August 5, 1885, to Martha Bernays. *Letters*, pp. 164f. Freud takes visible pleasure in telling this story which, considering the persons involved, has the air of an edifying and somewhat ironic fairy tale.

[86] He named his youngest daughter Anna after Anna Hammerschlag, his old teacher's only daughter; his two other daughters were also named after Jewish ladies of Freud's circle—Sophie, after a niece of Hammerschlag and Mathilda, after Frau Breuer. On the other hand, and perhaps the contrast is not without significance, he chose the first names of his three sons "on the other side": Oliver after Oliver Cromwell, Jean-Martin after Charcot, and Ernst after the "terrifying" Brücke, for whom Freud never lost his admiration.

[87] In the next chapter, we shall see that dreams of ambition figure prominently in *The Interpretation of Dreams* and *The Psychopathology of Everyday Life*. He speaks directly of his ambitions in his accounts of his two evenings at Charcot's home, and even more clearly in the scarcely veiled ideas he associates with Charcot's daughter.

[88] "Address read at a meeting of the B'nai B'rith held on May 6, 1926, in honor of Freud's seventieth birthday in an-

swer to a laudatory speech by Professor Ludwig Braun," SE XX, p. 273.

[39] *Letters,* p. 395.

[40] Letter to Barbara Low of April 19, 1926. *Letters,* p. 428. This letter was written in English, but the *"geheimnisvoll"* (mysterious) of the German translation strikes us as more compatible with Freud's style and probable meaning than the "miraculous" of the original. In the following references we have substituted "mysterious" for "miraculous." David Eder was an outstanding Zionist leader. Recruited by Haim Weizmann to be the first diplomatic representative of the Zionist executive in Jerusalem, he had formulated a policy of rapprochement with the Arabs. See Walter Laqueur, *Histoire du Sionisme* (Paris, 1973), pp. 268–69, 488, 501, 502, 505, and 516.

[41] *Origins,* p. 217. Letter of September 1, 1897.

[42] *Origins,* p. 258. Letter of July 7, 1898.

[43] Letter of June 9, 1899. *Origins,* p. 281.

[44] Letter of July 3, 1899. *Letters,* pp. 283f. "And what is your fiancée like, Uncle Jonas?" "Well, that's a matter of taste, but personally I don't like her," Uncle Jonas replies. This story, which evidently tickled Freud, recurs three or four times with slight variations in his letters to Fliess.

[45] At that time he thought of getting up an anthology of Jewish jokes, and reported to Fliess on the progress of his collection. The anthology was never published, but provided the greater part of the material used in *The Psychopathology of Everyday Life.*

[46] Oral statement reported by Jones, Vol. III, p. 221 (wording slightly modified). The executive committee of the Vienna Psychoanalytical Society decided that the Society's headquarters should be transferred to whatever city Freud settled in. All those present were Jews except Richard Sterba. Laughing, Freud pointed a finger at him, to indicate that he was an exception. Sterba, however, decided to share the fate of his Jewish colleagues and rejected the offers of

the German analysts who wished to make him director of the Vienna Institute and Clinic.

[47] Letter of Ernst Freud of May 12, 1938. *Letters*, p. 442: "I sometimes compare myself to the old Jacob who, when a very old man, was taken by his children to Egypt . . ."

[48] Letter to N.N. of December 14, 1937. *Letters*, p. 439.

[49] We have no means of knowing whether Freud had read Heinrich Graetz, Zunz, and the rationalist authors who contributed to the development of reform Judaism. It seems reasonable to suppose, however, that he would have had no difficulty in following Graetz in his condemnation of the Cabala. Believing as he did that the authentic Jewish spirit had always sided with reason in its struggle against obscurantism, Freud would naturally have regarded the esoteric Cabala as a foreign borrowing, leading to a deviation, not to say a perversion, of the traditional current. In this sense, he would merit Gershom Scholem's criticism of Graetz and his school (cf. *Judaica*, Frankfurt 1963, reprinted 1968, especially "Wissenschaft vom Judentum einst and jetzt," pp. 147–64), if not for the fact that instead of treating religious phenomena abstractly like the rationalists, he employed reason itself to expose the appeal of irrationality.

[50] Letter of February 18, 1929 to Arnold Zweig. *Freud/A. Zweig Letters*, pp. 3ff.

[51] On the turning inward that led Freud to lose interest in politics, see Carl E. Schorske, "Politics and Patricide in Freud's Interpretation of Dreams," *The American Historical Review*, LXXVIII: 2 (April 1973), pp. 328ff.

[52] It is not so self-evident as we might suppose in the light of what has happened since then that Freud should have regarded the man whom the Viennese affectionately called *"der schöne Karl"* as a personal enemy. The Austrian Jews were not unanimous in the condemnation of Lueger; many refused to take his demagogy seriously, for one thing because it had no great practical effect on them. In the next chapter we shall see, moreover, that the situation of the Jews

in what was then Austro-Hungary is still subject to controversy. According to some authors, the Jews on the whole were better off than other minorities; according to others, their situation was flourishing; Hannah Arendt, for example, maintains that the anti-Semitism of the Austrian Christian Social movement "remained without consequences; the decades during which Lueger ruled Vienna were actually a kind of golden age for the Jews." Hannah Arendt, *The Origins of Totalitarianism* (New Edition, New York, 1966), p. 44.

[53] There is no documentary evidence of the meeting between Freud and Herzl to which certain authors allude vaguely (cf. in particular, André Rousseau, *L'Influence de la tradition spéculative juive sur la pensée de Sigmund Freud et la génèse de son oeuvre.* Unpublished doctoral thesis, Paris, 1963). We do know, however, that he went to see Max Nordau in Paris, found him "vain and stupid" and made no attempt to see him again. Cf. Jones, I, p. 188.

[54] Letter of May 8, 1929, to Israel Spanier Wechsler. *Letters*, p. 387. Wechsler had asked him to donate his manuscripts to the Hebrew University.

[55] They had perhaps been based in part on a statement of Haim Weizmann to Jones, who had passed it on to Freud. Weizmann was reported to have said "that immigrants from Galicia arrived there with no clothes, but with copies of *Das Kapital* and *Die Traumdeutung* under their arms." Still according to Jones, "Freud held the great Zionist leader in the highest esteem." Jones III, pp. 30 and 234.

[56] Letter of February 18, 1928, to Enrico Morselli. *Letters*, p. 365. Here Freud shows that he was by no means the uncompromising doctrinaire that some people choose to see in him. As in the above-cited letter to A. A. Roback, he again, in the name of the Jewish people, thanks a man who has grieved him personally by failing to understand his ideas.

[57] *Freud/A. Zweig Letters*, p. 40. Letter of May 8, 1932, to Arnold Zweig. [Translation slightly modified.] Freud was not yet thinking of his Moses, but there is no doubt that his

correspondence with Arnold Zweig, which was very active at the time, contributed to rekindling or kindling his interest in Palestine and hence in the prophet.

[58] Letter of March 30, 1922, quote in Jones III, p. 83f. [There are manifest impossibilities in Jones's version of this letter. Marthe Robert in her French translation has tried to make it intelligible, and I have made comparable changes in the English.—R.M.]

[59] Just as in Berlin, Vienna, or Prague, the language of the Jews of that generation was never very far from Yiddish, so their manners, tastes, and habits of thought remained very close to their popular origins. Kafka explained this to the Jewish businessmen who in 1912 came to hear him speak on the Yiddish language and literature: they imagined, he said, that they no longer understood the "jargon," but they were mistaken; Yiddish was still alive in them, as was their Jewishness under their bourgeois German exteriors. Cf. "An Introductory Talk on the Yiddish Language" (delivered at an evening of recitations by the Jewish actor Isak Löwy at the Jewish Town Hall in Prague on February 18, 1912), in Franz Kafka, *Dearest Father*, New York, 1964, pp. 381ff.

[60] See *The Interpretation of Dreams*, SE IV, p. 195.

[61] At about the same time as he joined the B'nai B'rith (1897) Freud began a collection of Jewish stories, no doubt to serve as material for what was to become *Jokes and their Relation to the Unconscious* (SE VIII). See *Origins*, p. 211.

[62] Letter of December 3, 1885, to Minna Bernays. *Letters*, pp. 187f.

[63] Letter of August 29, 1883, to Martha Bernays. *Letters*, pp. 5of.

[64] On Freud's poverty, cf. the letters to Martha Bernays between 1882 and 1886, in *Letters*, pp. 7–218. At that time he was always short of money; often he could not afford to buy stationery, the slightest trip was a problem, and for want of money he feared that he would not be presentable at

Charcot's famous dinner party. Even after achieving fame, he went through periods of financial straits, and far from being wealthy at the time when he emigrated he was unable to pay the ransom demanded by the Nazis (the money was raised by Princess Marie Bonaparte).

[65] Letter of October 19, 1885, to Martha Bernays. *Letters*, pp. 172f. Mitzi was Freud's sister Marie, who had been obliged by the family's poverty to accept a position as governess.

[66] Letter of February 2, 1886, to Martha Bernays. *Letters*, p. 202.

[67] Letter of February 7, 1931, to Stefan Zweig. *Letters*, p. 402. Zweig's essay deals with Freud, Mesmer, and Mary Baker Eddy.

[68] Letter to Lou Andreas-Salomé of July 28, 1929. *Letters*, p. 390. Here Freud expresses the perhaps unjust, perhaps partly justified belief that Thomas Mann had written the article less because he had looked seriously into the subject than because he needed to publish something on Romanticism and psychoanalysis offered a new approach. (Cf. Thomas Mann, "Die Stellung Freuds in der modernen Geistesgeschichte," 1929.)

[69] Paradoxically, it was in his scientific pursuits that Freud departed most radically from the spirit of moderation by which he thought himself guided; witness his frivolity in the matter of cocaine, his enthusiasm for hypnotism, and in later years his interest in telepathy and the obstinacy with which he defended the theories of Lamarck. It is true that without these excursions beyond the frontiers of official medicine psychoanalysis would probably not have been born.

[70] Letter of February 2, 1886, to Martha Bernays. *Letters*, p. 202: "As I moved up into the favored position of head boy, where I remained for years and was in general trusted, people no longer had any reason to complain about me."

[71] The key to this riddle is provided by a letter to Martha in which Freud speaks of his friend Silberstein. Unbeknownst

to all, he had learned Spanish with this childhood friend, of whom he was very fond. The two boys had even amused themselves "by writing in Spanish a number of pieces that must still exist somewhere among my old papers." Letter of February 7, 1884. *Letters*, p. 97. [Translation slightly modified.]

[72] His utter lack of comprehension for Surrealism is well known. In general he was without understanding for modern art. In literature he never went beyond Thomas Mann and Arthur Schnitzler. Even from the psychoanalytical point of view, Impressionism and the avant-garde movements did not arouse his curiosity. There is real anger in the letter he wrote Karl Abraham when Abraham, meaning no doubt to give him pleasure, sent him his own portrait by a "modern" artist of his acquaintance. "I know what an admirable person you are, which makes it the more shattering that such a cruel penalty should have to be exacted for such a trivial blot on your character as your tolerance or sympathy for modern 'art.'" *Freud/Abraham Letters*, p. 332.

[73] See Klaus Wagenbach, *Franz Kafka: eine Biographie seiner Jugend*, 1883–1912, Francke, 1958, pp. 35ff.

[74] Wagenbach, op. cit., pp. 34–64.

[75] Cf. Note 27, above, Gustav Landauer's letter to Mauthner.

[76] Cf. Wagenbach, op. cit., pp. 37f.

[77] In connection with the secondary schooling of Alexander Ulyanov (Lenin's brother), Trotsky wrote: "The chief implement of torture was the classics. 'The study of the ancient languages,' explained the creators of the educational system, 'because of the very difficulty of mastering them, inculcates modesty, and modesty is the foremost attribute and the foremost requirement of a genuine education.' The classics were called on to play the role of ball and chain fastened onto the child's intellect." The author notes, incidentally, that while Alexander was morally crushed by the system, Vladimir Ilyich, who was also at the head of his class, was

able, thanks to his rugged constitution, to absorb all this dead weight without harm. Cf. Leon Trotsky, *The Young Lenin* (Doubleday & Company, Inc., New York, 1972, p. 39. Tr. Max Eastman).

[78] This insidious form of mystification is one of the themes of social criticism that Kafka develops in *The Castle*, not overtly, but in conformity with the occult character of the phenomenon, under the cover of a pseudo-odyssey, whose heroes are the gods of Olympus transformed into all-powerful bureaucrats at the head of an organization that was as formidable as it was invisible (one of the Gentlemen of the Castle is named Momus like the Greek god of mockery). Cf. Marthe Robert, *L'Ancien et le Nouveau* (Paris, 1963), and Franz Kafka, *Briefe*, op. cit., letter to Max Brod postmarked August 7, 1920, pp. 279ff. Kafka's radical critique of humanism was one of the things that made him unintelligible to a Marxist author like Lukacs. When it comes to revealing the ties between humanism and upper-class ideology, the Marxist "demystifiers" are as timid as Freud.

[79] "Some Reflections on Schoolboy Psychology," SE XIII, pp. 241f. [Translation slightly modified.]

[80] An obvious allusion to the liberal atmosphere prevailing in Freud's *Gymnasium*, where, as we have seen, there was no racial problem at the time.

[81] For Freud his love of antiquity was not one of those enthusiasms that commit one to nothing, but a true religion, involving sacrifices and ritual acts, such as the search for relics and pilgrimages to the holy cities of Rome and Athens. His sacrifices were heavy from the financial point of view, for at the time when he began to put his religion into practice (about 1895), rare objects and trips to Rome were luxuries he could ill afford (in his letter to Stefan Zweig, quoted in Note 21, Chapter 2, above, he writes: ". . . despite my much vaunted frugality I have sacrificed a great deal for my collection of Greek, Roman and Egyptian antiquities.").

[82] On Jacob Bernays, son of the Hamburg *haham* and

Freud's uncle by marriage, cf. A. Momigliano, *Jacob Bernays* (Amsterdam and London, 1969). (I wish to thank Pierre Vidal-Naquet for calling my attention to this monograph.) In 1932 Freud wrote to Arnold Zweig: "As it happens, I am able to send you something from us today. I had a hand in editing the book which is going off to you at the same time as this. They are the letters of an uncle of my wife's who was a famous classical scholar and, it appears, an outstanding personality. His attitude toward the Jewish and Christian faiths is worthy of attention. Also his affectionate relationship with Paul Heyse. I beg you to read this little book." *Freud/A. Zweig Letters*, p. 48. Letter of November 27, 1932, to Arnold Zweig. The book in question is *Jacob Bernays, Ein Lebensbild in Briefen* (Breslau, 1932). Unfortunately I have been unable to procure a copy. According to Momigliano Bernays found no difficulty in reconciling his passion for classical learning with strict Jewish orthodoxy, while Mauthner had broken not only with the Jewish religion, but also with Judaism as a form of thought and culture.

[83] Heinrich Heine, Letter from Helgoland of July 29, 1830. See *Juden und Judentum*, p. 380.

[84] On Heine's return to the Bible, see Ludwig Rosenthal, *Heinrich Heine als Jude* (Ullstein, Frankfurt, Berlin, Vienna, 1973), pp. 281–320.

[85] Cf. the passage from Freud's letter to Romain Rolland quoted above.

[86] We are in the dark as to the real value of the ancient art objects that Freud began to collect at the time of his "splendid isolation" and kept adding to all his life. If a valuation was ever made, it has not been published. It seems likely that the pieces were less valuable for their rarity and beauty than for the role they played in Freud's inner life. Fliess, a cultivated man but apparently more skeptical than Freud, sometimes chided Freud on the subject of his "disgusting old idols," something none of Freud's disciples (many of whom

enriched the collection by donating their "finds") would have dared to do.

III. AMBITION THWARTED

1 "By one of those obscure routes behind the official consciousness the old man's death affected me deeply. I valued him highly and understood him very well indeed, and with his peculiar mixtures of deep wisdom and imaginative light-heartedness he meant a great deal in my life. By the time he died his life had long been over, but at a death the whole past stirs within one." Letter of November 2, 1896. *Origins,* p. 170. These few rather commonplace lines in which Freud informs Fliess of his loss give no inkling of the "Oedipean" dream that would soon lead Freud to treat himself like one of his patients.

2 The English translation of the title (*The Interpretation of Dreams*) and the two French translations, *La Science des rêves* and *L'Interprétation des rêves,* all fail to convey Freud's intention. The German word *Traumdeutung* means specifically "dream book," one of those cheap booklets sold at fairs or from door to door and bought in quantity by women of the lower classes—by "cooks," says Freud. Before Freud, the word had no other meaning. Thus there was nothing scientific or pedantic about the title, as might be supposed when it is broken down into its two elements; on the contrary, it evokes the age-old superstitious belief that dreams offer a symbolic key to the future. In all likelihood Freud chose it deliberately, no doubt with a trace of malice, since in a measure his book supports primitive folk beliefs—which at least have the advantage of seeing in dreams a meaning related to the life of the dreamer—in opposition to the stubborn skepticism of his enlightened contemporaries. With this provocative title, he flung a challenge at the specialists and called upon them to show a little more humility. That is why I refer to it by the German title in the text of this chapter.

[3] For Freud's account of the dream, see *The Interpretation of Dreams*, SE IV, pp. 107ff. The interpretation is scattered throughout the book; it is the central exhibit in Freud's demonstration, and he returns to it in almost every chapter to illustrate both his empirical method and the various points of the theory in which it culminated.

[4] In support of his decision to keep silent, he often cited a passage from Goethe's *Faust:* "Das Beste, was Du wissen kanns/Wirst Du den Buben doch nicht sagen" (Surely you won't impart the best part of your knowledge to those dolts).

[5] "I stand for an infinitely freer sexual life, although I myself have made little use of such freedom." Letter of July 8, 1915, to James J. Putnam. *Letters*, p. 308.

[6] His own children knew nothing about the romance of his engagement until 1953, when the first volume of Jones's biography, containing extracts from Freud's letters to Martha Bernays, appeared. His subsequent love life remained equally secret; he was suspected of intimacy with his sister-in-law Minna, who lived in his house, and later was thought to have been in love with Lou Andreas-Salomé, but he himself never said or did anything to support these suppositions.

[7] In *Les Vases communicants* (Paris, 1932), Appendix, pp. 200–7, André Breton accuses Freud of pusillanimity, for having censored his dreams. But could Freud have done otherwise without gravely imperiling his domestic happiness and peace of mind?

[8] It is too often forgotten that the late nineteenth century was the heyday of sexology. Yet neither Havelock Ellis nor Krafft-Ebing ever created a scandal. It is true that their views on sex were not Freud's; they were acceptable since, by concentrating on perversion, they tended to reinforce the existing taboos rather than to surmount them.

[9] Freud expresses surprise and indignation (especially in *An Autobiographical Study*, SE XX) that the public should have been shocked at his saying out loud what Charcot, the

gynecologist Chrobak, and many others had said more discreetly, and especially that prominent figures whose authority he felt justified in evoking had disavowed him. He mistook the nature of the taboo, which was less concerned with the reality of sex than with what was said on the subject.

10 "I have avoided sex, but 'dirt' is unavoidable and begs to be treated with indulgence." Letter of September 6, 1899. *Origins*, p. 295. [Translation slightly modified.]

11 Later on, Freud realized how paradoxical it was that the *Traumdeutung* should make a secret of his idea, central to his whole theory, of the dominant role of psycho-sexuality. He tried to explain this anomaly in a note added to Chapter VII of the book: "What governed my decision was simply my seeing that an explanation of sexual dreams would involved me deeply in the still unsolved problems of perversion and bisexuality, and I accordingly reserved this material for another occasion." (*The Interpretation of Dreams*, SE V, pp. 606f., note 2.) This is in contradiction with the above-quoted letter to Fliess, where he admits that he avoided the questions not for theoretical but for moral reasons.

12 The failure of Freud's work with cocaine left him with prolonged bitterness; in his *Autobiographical Study* (SE XX), he attributes his failure to his fiancée, and the theme recurs constantly in the dreams recorded in the *Traumdeutung*. On his scientific research, see Didier Anzieu, *l'Autoanalyse* (Paris, 1959). According to Anzieu, Freud was an excellent observer but a mediocre experimenter.

13 Breuer was a typical product of the strait-laced Jewish environment that Freud had broken away from only partly and recently, and that is why the conflict between the two men ended so badly; Breuer embodied the strict traditional morality to which Freud still clung but from which he knew he would have to free himself if he wished to surmount his failures.

[14] We shall have more to say of this "My friend R. was my uncle" dream (*The Interpretation of Dreams*, SE IV, pp. 137ff.), here referred to as the professor-dream, in which cynical careerism takes a particularly revolting form. Freud unquestionably needed courage to bare his "villainy" to the Vienna "philistines," who must have been aware of his situation and his vain efforts to gain a professorship. Nevertheless, as we shall see, the dream was not directed against the philistines, but against the Jewish colleagues from whom Freud unconsciously wished to dissociate himself.

[15] Letter of March 15, 1898. *Origins*, p. 248.

[16] *The Interpretation of Dreams*, SE IV, p. 192.

[17] Cf. David Bakan, *Freud et la tradition mystique juive*, and the above-cited (Chapter 2, Note 53) thesis of André Rousseau, which describes Freud's situation as if the Nazis had occupied Vienna in 1880. This anachronism provides a more dramatic picture but also makes the dream published in the *Traumdeutung* absolutely incomprehensible.

[18] Joachim Remak, "The Healthy Invalid: How Doomed Was the Hapsburg Empire?" *Journal of Modern History* (June 1969). Remak cites the case of Martin Freud, who enlisted as soon as war was declared in 1914 despite a leg wound that would have won him a deferment. After all, he said to his father, how could he turn down an opportunity to enter Russia without having to change his religion? Cf., especially for the Lueger period, Hannah Arendt, *The Origins of Totalitarianism* (New York, 1966), p. 44.

[19] Jones, Vol. II, p. 171. [Translation slightly modified.]

[20] The candidate had to apply to two of his colleagues, who proposed his name to the Faculty Council. If the Council reported favorably, the nomination was submitted to the Minister, and the Minister had it signed by the Emperor.

[21] Letter of March 11, 1902. *Origins*, p. 344. One is struck by Freud's unaccustomed exuberance at the news of his appointment: "The public enthusiasm is immense. Congratulations and bouquets keep pouring in, as if the role of sexu-

ality had suddenly been recognized by His Majesty, the interpretation of dreams confirmed by the Council of Ministers, and the necessity of psycho-analytic therapy of hysteria carried by a two-third majority in Parliament." Schorske, "Politics and Patricide . . ." See Chapter II, note 5, notes the use of hackneyed metaphors in this passage, as though Freud associated his first triumph with his early childhood ambitions. This letter incidentally is his last communication to Fliess, except for a postcard with a view of the temple of Neptune at Paestum.

22 Freud himself felt that his tendency to overwork and his obsession with achieving fame by a great discovery were typical of the half-assimilated Jew. In September 1883, he wrote to Martha, who was worried about his overworking: "I would rather renounce my ambition, attract less attention, have less success than endanger my nervous system. In the future, for the remainder of my apprenticeship in the hospital, I think I shall try to live more like the Goyim—modestly, learning and practising the usual things and not striving after discoveries and delving too deep." (*Letters*, p. 54.) [Translation slightly modified.] And a little later he told her the story of Benedikt Stilling who, too poor to devote himself entirely to research, resigned himself to practicing medicine: "But for thirteen years he worked every morning on the human spinal cord, the result of which was a great work, and every evening he continued to work on the brain, and he is known as the foremost among the scientists to whom we owe the knowledge of this noble organ. All this shows the industry, the tenacious enthusiasm of the Jew. . . . This we too can do." *Letters*, p. 71. [Translation slightly modified.]

23 Freud's admiration for Cromwell was much more than a passing youthful infatuation. It was in Cromwell's honor that he named his second son Oliver.

24 "Some Reflections on Schoolboy Psychology," SE XIII, p. 242.

25 Freud's feeling about science is most eloquently revealed

in his admirable obituary of Charcot, written in 1893. ". . . he would recall the myth of Adam, who, when God brought the creatures of Paradise before him to be distinguished and named, may have experienced to the fullest degree that intellectual enjoyment which Charcot praised so highly." "Charcot," SE III, p. 13.

[26] Brücke was on terms of close friendship with Emil Du Bois-Reymond, Hermann Helmholtz, and Carl Ludwig. In their youth these men had founded a scientific group to defend their ideas. Du Bois-Reymond wrote in 1842: "Brücke and I swore a solemn oath to impose the following truth: 'No other forces than the common physical-chemical ones are active within the organism. In those cases which cannot for the moment be explained by these forces one has to find the specific mode or form of their action . . .'" (Quoted by Jones, I, p. 40.) [English slightly modified here.] Despite the unexpected methods to which his own discoveries led him, Freud was strongly marked to the very end by this Brücke-Helmholtz creed. In *The Interpretation of Dreams*, Freud himself makes the Brücke-bridge pun, though only in passing, without going into its implications. Brücke is one of the key characters in the *Traumdeutung*, appearing frequently in the record of Freud's dreams or in the associations developed from them.

[27] Fleischl-Marxow fascinated Freud as much by his elegance and charm as by his talents as a scientist. At the age of twenty-five, while directing certain experiments in pathology, he had contracted an infectious disease. His thumb was amputated, but the continued growth of neuromas necessitated further operations, so that his life become a long torment and slow death. Freud tried to cure him with the cocaine and morphine to which he was then habituated. The treatment did Fleischl-Marxow no good but considerably hastened his end. Freud's feelings of love, hate, envy, pity and guilt toward this exceptional man play a large part in the *Traumdeutung*.

[28] Letter of October 25, 1883, to Martha. *Letters*, p. 73, 74.

29 The letters to Martha show how lost Freud felt during his stay in Paris. Plagued by his eternal poverty, he also suffered from his awkwardness, his stilted manners, and provincial appearance. He was so terrified at the prospect of his first visit to Charcot's home, so afraid of committing a blunder that he took cocaine before going. But in the end he carried it off very well and immediately saw everything in a more agreeable light. He was so full of Mademoiselle Charcot's praises that Martha seems to have been somewhat jealous, perhaps with some justification in view of the welter of ambitions that were then warring within him. In that period of disarray, he may indeed have toyed with vague ideas of a wealthy marriage. One indication of this may be found in *The Psychopathology of Everyday Life* (SE VI, pp. 148f.), where he analyzes an error of memory, which at first sight seemed inexplicable. In writing one of the last chapters of *The Interpretation of Dreams* (SE V, p. 535), Freud quoted Alphonse Daudet's *Le Nabab* from memory. In his recollection the hero was a poor bookkeeper named Jocelyn who while strolling one day in Paris saved a person of importance from a serious accident by stopping a runaway horse. In rereading the book Freud saw to his dismay that the bookkeeper's name was not Jocelyn but Joyeuse, and that the novel contained no such scene as he had imagined. Thus it was he himself, Monsieur *Joyeuse* (*Freud* in German) who had imagined the whole story in order that a person of importance might say to him: "You are my savior. I owe my life to you. What can I do for you?" (SE VI, p. 149.) This rescue daydream, which he analyzed later as an element in the "family novel"—usually the savior marries the daughter of the person of importance—is quite in keeping with his state of mind at the time when Charcot seemed to be offering him his support and when, like Daudet's M. Joyeuse, he daydreamed while strolling sadly through the streets of the capital (it was at Charcot's that he made the acquaintance of Daudet).

30 Freud's identification with Goethe is striking. In his analysis of a passage in *Dichtung und Wahrheit* [Goethe's autobi-

ography], he observed that a man who was his mother's favorite son (his own case) could not fail. And he never missed an opportunity to mention his own name side by side with Goethe's.

IV. YOU ARE REQUESTED TO CLOSE THE EYES

[1] Josef Popper-Lynkeus, "Träumen wie Wachen," in *Phantasien eines Realisten* (Vienna, 1899). On Freud's relations with Popper-Lynkeus, cf. "Josef Popper-Lynkeus and the Theory of Dreams," SE XIX, pp. 261ff.

[2] This memorable "first" occurred at the Belle Vue private sanatorium in the suburbs of Vienna, where the Freud family spent its summer holidays from 1895 to 1900. Half in earnest and half in jest, Freud wondered some years later if the place might not some day be graced by a commemorative tablet, saying: "In this house on July 24, 1895, the Secret of Dreams was Revealed to Dr. Sigmund Freud." *Origins*, p. 322, letter of June 12, 1900, to Fliess. Although Freud kept Fliess informed of all his discoveries, he did not tell him of the Irma dream in writing, but first mentioned it in the published book. This dream, incidentally, is not the first dream that Freud analyzed; by 1895 he had undoubtedly analyzed some of his patients' dreams, but he did not then think it possible to publish them without breach of professional secrecy. In 1900 he was still hesitating; then he resolved to publish only his own dreams, but this did not obviate the main difficulty, for in his very small social set, physicians and patients were often close friends. Even five years later Irma might have taken umbrage at the role she plays in Freud's interpretation, for she and other characters in the dream were easily recognizable under their false names.

[3] Didier Anzieu, *L'Autoanalyse*, op. cit., p. 29. Anzieu's arguments are convincing: Irma like Anna was a widow; she was close enough to the Freud family to be invited to a reception given by Martha three days later on the occasion of

her thirty-fourth birthday; lastly, Freud provides an unquestionable indication of her identity by saying that the word "ananas"—which came to his mind in the course of his associations—was related phonetically to his patient's last name. One need only substitute "first name" for "last name" to determine Irma's probable identity. Anzieu also notes the extraordinary role of widows and death in this story, whose most realistic features are raised to the level of mythology.

[4] Letter of May 24, 1895. *Origins*, p. 120. [Translation slightly modified.] Fliess believed he had discovered a law making it possible to determine the periods most and least favorable to fecundation. Alluding to his wife's pregnancy, Freud wrote to him: "For me your discovery is a few months too late, but it may come in handy next year." Anzieu infers that this last child, who was to be called Wilhelm in honor of Fliess, or, if it was a girl, Anna, was not exactly wanted. This is quite possible and would help us to understand the peculiar atmosphere of the Irma dream and Freud's ill-concealed animosity toward Martha (in the dream).

[5] Letter to Martha, quoted by Jones, I, p. 90. "I admire and love him with an intellectual passion, if you will allow me such a phrase. His destruction will move me as the destruction of a sacred and famous temple would have affected an ancient Greek. I love him not so much as a human being, but as one of nature's precious achievements." In the *Traumdeutung* Freud denies having prescribed injections of cocaine to help Fleischl overcome the effects of morphine, and says he prescribed it in the form of a powder to be breathed.

[6] Freud speaks of Nathan Weiss's suicide in a long letter vibrant with emotion, which is a precious source of information on the Jewish community of Vienna at that time and its more or less specific diseases (mainly tuberculosis and suicide, as shown by the frequent tragedies in Freud's circle). Freud paints an impressive picture of the Weiss family, with the sense of detail and literary talent which he would later put into his case histories. He describes the father, a learned rabbi, proud, miserly, and malignant, and the brilliantly

gifted son, a seductive, cynical careerist, who quite unexpectedly went to pieces just as he was about to attain his goal (a rich marriage). In his letter Freud makes no secret of what both fascinated and repelled him in the character of this Jewish parvenu who, with no other talent than that of his narcissism, managed to disguise his self-destructive drive as an "extraordinary appetite for life." Letter to Martha of September 16, 1883. *Letters*, pp. 59–65.

7 On the cocaine episode, see Jones I, pp. 78–97, and Freud, "An Autobiographical Study," SE XX, pp. 14f.

8 Freud says nothing, either in his record of the dream or in his interpretation, of this "solution." Its nature can probably be inferred, however, from his ideas on the etiology of hysteria and of anxiety neuroses. The latter, he believed, were caused by total or partial sexual privation, and his letters to Fliess show the importance he attached to this part of his theory. If Irma was indeed Anna Hammerschlag, she had been a widow for nine years. Presumably Freud had advised her to remarry, or to take a lover, a suggestion which in so puritanical a family can only have elicited a scandalized refusal.

9 From a modern point of view, Freud's reluctance to divulge the base thoughts connected with his ambition would seem more justified than his evasiveness in sexual matters. It took a great deal of courage to surmount this reluctance even in part; and throughout the *Traumdeutung* we see how much it pained him, despite his familiarity with the "villainies" of the unconscious, to find such blackness in his own soul and even more so to have to reveal it to the public.

10 Letter of November 2, 1896. *Origins*, p. 171.

11 The English (like the French) translation reads: "in slightly different terms" instead of "in greater detail," doubtless to take account of the actual character of the two texts. (SE IV, p. 317f.)

12 "*Man bittet*," instead of "*Man wird gebeten*" as in the letter.

13 *"Ein Auge zudrücken,"* "to close one eye"=to look the other way, to overlook, to show indulgence for someone's faults. *"Die Augen zudrücken"*=to close one's own or some-one else's eyes, here the eyes of the dead.

14 SE IV, p. 318.

15 Freud did everything in his power to prevent Marie Bonaparte from buying this correspondence, which after his break with Fliess he no doubt thought too outspoken. We can be sure that he would never have consented to its publication.

16 *Origins*, p. 171.

17 *The Interpretation of Dreams*, SE IV, p. 137.

18 *The Interpretation of Dreams*, SE IV, p. 138.

19 Ibid., SE IV, p. 138, Note 1. [Translation slightly modified.]

20 Freud's attitude toward this "unfortunate" uncle may have accounted in some measure for his feelings toward the numerous Josefs who played a part in his life: Josef Paneth ("my friend Josef" mentioned in the *Traumdeutung*); Josef Breuer, whom he admired and loved until doctrinal divergencies put an end to their friendship and who, by preparing the way for psychoanalysis, played an essential role in his life; Josef Popper-Lynkeus, author of a book on dreams published in 1899, in whom Freud recognized a precursor of his own ideas and a man of great intellectual courage; and finally the biblical Joseph, with whom he openly identified himself in the *Traumdeutung* because like him he was son of Jacob and like him a past master in the art of explaining dreams.

21 Here Freud gives an example of his extraordinary faculty of association, which, especially in the period under discussion, did much to convince him of the soundness of his view of psychological determinism. When about to leave Paris in February 1866, he was offered two positions, one in Berlin, the other in Breslau; he had not yet decided between them. Though the context did not seem to favor such an associa-

tion, the mere mention of Breslau sufficed to remind him of the problem of his heredity—a painful problem which no doubt had a good deal to do with his choice of Berlin.

[22] Letter of February 10, 1886. *Letters*, p. 210.

[23] Ibid.

[24] *The Interpretation of Dreams*, SE IV, p. 193. [Translation slightly modified.]

[25] In the last chapter I shall speak at length of this kind of psychic production which Freud early found in his patients (he already had a profound knowledge of it in 1897, though at that time he regarded it merely as a morbid symptom, an expression of paranoia), and referred to it as "family novel of the neurotic," so taking into account both its novelistic structure and its main content, i.e., the patient's relation to his family. At a certain stage in his development the child becomes disappointed with his parents and gives himself an imaginary family which he places as high as possible in the human and social hierarchy. He is the son of a royal or divine pair; or of a nobleman, by whom the child's mother was seduced. In this way the child satisfies his "Oedipean" desires and above all his megalomaniacal pride, for by disavowing his real family he sets himself free for an extraordinary destiny; now he can become whatever he chooses, a prophet, a savior, a saint, or an all-powerful leader. Later on, when he begins to recognize the principle of reality, he may content himself with being a great, or merely, successful, man. On the many implications of this infantile megalomania, see Marthe Robert, *Roman des origines et origines du roman*, Paris, 1972.

[26] The disjointedness of Freud's analyses does not result solely from the technical requirements of exposition; it is also a means of concealment, but not entirely successful as such, for it is possible to fit the pieces together accurately enough to complete the interpretation without recourse to extraneous elements.

[27] Freud returns to the theme of parents' debts to their chil-

dren in another famous dream, the "dream of the table d'hôte." *On Dreams*, SE V, pp. 636–640. Here, as so often, he invokes Goethe. In the two lines quoted—"You bring us into the world" and "Let the poor man fall into debt"— Freud plays on the double meaning of the word *Schuld*, which means both debt and guilt.

28 Ibid.

29 *On Dreams*, SE V, p. 652.

30 The "revolutionary dream" has been brilliantly studied by Carl E. Schorske ("Politics and Patricide . . ." see Chapter II, Note 51) who regards it as proof that Freud had a diverted vocation for politics. In this there is some truth, but it might be more accurate to say that for him politics was merely one of the numerous careers that might have attracted his ambition.

31 For this story and the interpretation of the "revolutionary dream" see *The Interpretation of Dreams*, SE IV, pp. 298ff., 233, and SE V, pp. 432 and 470.

32 At the time of the *Traumdeutung* the study of megalomania conceived in relation to anal and urethral eroticism was in its beginnings. Freud's knowledge of the matter was purely empirical.

33 *The Interpretation of Dreams*, SE IV, pp. 194ff.

34 Obviously it is not for us to fill in the gaps, an undertaking that would call for hazardous inferences or pure invention.

35 In a sense the vision of Freud's "Roman" dreams was truly prophetic, for after undermining the edifice of Christian ethics, Freud succeeded in revolutionizing the Western world with his Jewish law.

36 This dream of the "Promised Land" is the first document in which Freud openly identifies himself with Moses. In what is conceivably an earlier example Moses is not mentioned by name, and for lack of information one can only conjecture. I am referring to one of those *"Fehlleistungen,"*

the theory of which Freud sketched at roughly the same time as he was working on the *Traumdeutung*. It is analyzed very succinctly, not in the *Psychopathology of Everyday Life* but only in a letter to Fliess of August 26, 1898 (*Origins*, p. 261), in which Freud speaks of it as too intimate to be made public. After trying in vain to remember the name of the author of *Andreas Hofer*, the poet Julius Mosen, which he knew perfectly well, he discovered the reasons for his forgetfulness. "The Julius had not slipped my memory. I was able to prove (i) that I had repressed the name Mosen because of certain associations; (ii) that material from my infancy played a part in the repression . . ." Julius was in fact the name of a younger brother whom he had detested and who, as though in response to Sigmund's wishes, had died young, a fact that had left Sigmund with an intense feeling of guilt. As for Mosen, the resemblance to Moses permits one to conjecture with Anzieu (*L'Autoanalyse*, p. 103) that the "certain associations" mentioned by Freud had to do with the Prophet. The hypothesis would be fragile if we did not know that Moses held an extraordinary fascination for Freud. We shall see wherein and why in our last chapter, in connection first with his essay on Michelangelo's *Moses*, and then with *Moses and Monotheism*, which book may be termed the culmination of his "family novel." Considering that forty years elapsed between 1898 when he failed to remember the name of Julius Mosen and dreamed of the Promised Land and 1938 when he completed this last book, we may say that Freud was obsessed with Moses for a good part of his life.

[37] See Carl E. Schorske ("Politics and Patricide," loc. cit.), who throws an interesting light on this much neglected aspect of the "Roman dreams."

[38] Here I draw on Carl E. Schorske, who in the above-mentioned article cites some highly convincing documents in support of his thesis regarding the relation between Freud and Winckelmann, in particular, a biography of Winckelmann by Carl Justi, the first edition of which appeared while

Freud was still at secondary school and the second in 1898, the year in which Freud became passionately interested in archaeology and had his "Roman dreams." Schorske writes: "The Justi biography reveals remarkable similarities between Winckelmann's life and intellectual stance and Freud's: poverty, an acute sense of low social status, failure to find a congenial intellectual position or adequate professional recognition, a string of intense friendships with homosexual overtones, hatred of political tyranny, hostility to organized religion, and a generativity crisis at the age of forty that resulted in a 'first work' of a new and revolutionary kind." ("Politics and Patricide . . ." *The American Historical Review* LXXVIII, p. 338, Note 28.)

[39] On the strength of these "Roman dreams," certain writers have maintained that Freud was really attracted by Catholicism, that his "Catholic nannie" exerted a profound influence on him in childhood and that he seriously considered conversion. This is unjustifiable. Neither Freud's nor anyone else's opinions can be inferred from dreams, since an opinion, strictly speaking, is nothing other than a desire to express oneself in words or acts. If I say that I believe one thing or another, you may think that I am mistaken, that my opinion is based on ignorance or unconscious motives of self-interest, but you are not entitled to doubt that what I have said is indeed my opinion and that I wish to be identified with the order of ideas it represents. Freud detested Christianity long before he invented psychoanalysis; he detested it as a Jew who had suffered from its power to oppress, and later on as a believer in reason, because he regarded it as an irrational survival, an archaeological vestige and a barrier to the progress of thought. He never wrote, said, or did anything to contradict this attitude. Thus he did not *express* the opinion that these writers impute to him. But did he perhaps hold it unconsciously? No. In the unconscious we find instinctive tendencies and desires, but not opinions. A man may desire unconsciously to be like his father, or to change his skin and name so as not to be like him, or to supplant him or in some sense to kill him, but he can-

not desire *unconsciously* to be a disciple of St. Augustine or Hegel. Freud's strange love affair with Rome is sufficiently explained by the mixture of attraction and repulsion he felt for the society and history of the Gentiles; what drew him unconsciously to Rome was not the Church, but his own ideas of grandeur and his suffering at being low-born.

[40] *The Interpretation of Dreams*, SE IV, p. 197.

[41] *The Psychopathology of Everyday Life*, SE VI, pp. 219f.

[42] *The Interpretation of Dreams*, SE IV, pp. 169ff. The analysis of the famous dream is continued in SE IV, pp. 180, 191, 281ff., 305 and SE V, p. 467.

[43] *The Interpretation of Dreams*, SE IV, p. 191.

[44] These errors, which appear in the first and sometimes in the second edition of the *Traumdeutung* relate without exception to Freud's relations with his father (we have dealt above with his substitution of Hasdrubal for Hamilcar). Most of them are analyzed by Freud himself in *The Psychopathology of Everyday Life*. Two such mistakes were pointed out by Fritz Wittels. These Freud merely rectified in subsequent editions of the book. The first, which slipped into his analysis of the "revolutionary dream," relates to the inscription on a medallion struck by the English to commemorate the destruction of the Spanish Armada. Freud recalls the inscription at the end of a long chain of associations, but according to Wittels, the text is incomplete: the name of Jehovah is missing. Irritated by this discovery by "an unsolicited biographer," Freud did not deny the omission but offered a very awkward explanation for it: "The English medallion bears the deity's name in Hebrew lettering on a cloud in the background. It is so placed that it can be taken as being part either of the design or of the inscription." *The Interpretation of Dreams*, SE IV, p. 214, Note 1. The second mistake pointed out by Wittels occurs in the analysis of the "Non vixit" dream, which we shall discuss further on. It concerns another inscription, that on the ped-

estal of the monument to the Emperor Joseph in Vienna. Ibid., SE V, p. 423, Note 1.

[45] *The Interpretation of Dreams*, SE V, p. 456, Note 2.

[46] Ibid.

[47] SE 5, 455ff. [Translation slightly modified.]

[48] *The Psychopathology of Everyday Life*, SE VI, p. 219.

[49] In his dream Freud sees the titles of two English books: *The Wealth of Nations* and Maxwell's *Matter and Motion*. *Matter and Motion* makes him think of Molière's *Le Malade Imaginaire*—is matter laudable (sic)—a *motion of bowels* (cf. *The Interpretation of Dreams*, SE V, p. 520). From this material, he tells us, the gap in the chain of associations, which prevents us from grasping the ultimate meaning of the dream, can easily be filled. "Easily" is too much said; but one can hardly doubt that this chain of associations, like the insults and humiliations with which the real traveler wishes to cover his two companions, relates to the anal erotic sphere (the clysters and "motion [movement] of the bowels" from *Le Malade Imaginaire*, modestly quoted in English). Thus placed in direct relation with fecal matter, the torn book in the dream of the "botanical monograph" about which Freud has not told us the whole story, may well have provided his father with an opportunity to show in words or in actions that printed paper can serve a purpose that has nothing to do with the intellect. In that case we should understand why the incident made so profound an impression on the child.

[50] *The Interpretation of Dreams*, SE V, pp. 441ff.

[51] Theodor Herzl, *Das neue Ghetto*, written in Paris in 1894 under the impact of the Dreyfus case.

[52] In the perspective of the present work I have not been specially concerned with the purely "Oedipean" aspect of the conflict. In any case, I would have had difficulty in finding material, for our documents, essentially *The Interpretation of Dreams*, the letters to Fliess, and *The Psychopathology of Everyday Life* are chary of details. In 1897

Freud wrote to Fliess: "I find that I too was in love with my mother and jealous of my father; this I now regard as a common phenomenon of early childhood." (Letter of October 15, 1897. *Origins*, p. 223.) [Translation slightly modified.] The words "I now regard" hardly suggest that he already looked upon the "Oedipus complex" as an established truth. Indeed, it was just beginning to make its appearance in his thinking and is not even mentioned in *The Interpretation of Dreams*. True, he mentions crucial childhood memories going back to the age of three, which throw light on certain aspects of his affective life. But in the main he avoids saying anything relating directly to his mother or even to his parents taken together as an image of married life. On one of the rare occasions when he finds himself in the presence of an "Oedipean couple"—in the Marburg-Schiller dream— he hides behind one of his patients, a sufferer from obsessional neurosis, so demonstrating that he would rather be regarded as slightly neurotic than divulge information that he considers too personal. Thus Amalia Freud is a rather colorless and disembodied figure in the *Traumdeutung*, unlike her husband whose features stand out with amazing clarity. One need only assemble the elements scattered throughout Freud's dreams to discover not only the living face of this Jewish father so curiously destined to incarnate all the fathers of the world, but also the society in which Freud moved at the time of his hardest struggles. In this sense the *Traumdeutung*, the masterwork that established a new science and new form of thought, is also something else to which Freud, in view of his scientific aim, could not have aspired: a precious document of the times, all the more instructive because it did not aim at objectivity.

53 *Origins*, letter of October 3, 1897, p. 219.

54 *Origins*, letter of October 23, 1898, p. 269.

55 *The Interpretation of Dreams*, SE V, p. 421. [Translation slightly modified.]

56 Ibid., SE V, p. 422.

57 *The Interpretation of Dreams*, SE IV, p. 214, Note 1.

⁵⁸ The most amusing of these is a dream in which Jakob Freud plays "a political role among the Magyars" after his death. Here Freud is obviously trying to make up for the wrong he has done his father by raising him to a high dignity, but in the course of analysis he is forced to admit that he has raised his father so high in order to make him fall to the lowest level of scatology: starting from a circle of heroic ideas woven around Garibaldi, he ends with the image of the dying man soiling himself. *The Interpretation of Dreams*, SE B, pp. 428ff.

⁵⁹ At that time the existence of Athens and the Acropolis was known to him only from books; he expected his journey to confirm their reality. But this is precisely where it failed, for rather than succeed in what his father had never been able to do—Jakob Freud had never traveled, and since he despised books, neither Athens nor the Acropolis meant anything to him—Freud preferred to remove the sacred edifice, the source of all the "other side's" light, from the face of the earth.

V. THE LAST NOVEL

¹ *Origins*, p. 223. [Translation slightly modified.]

² The term "Oedipean conflict"—as it is still called in the *Traumdeutung*—is used in the famous pages where Freud, struck by the resemblance between the infantile drama that he was able to reconstitute in all cases of neurosis and the tragic intrigue that is the subject of Sophocles' *Oedipus Rex* and more obscurely of Shakespeare's *Hamlet*, suggests that this is a universal fatality, but does not for the moment try to prove it. The association of the specific conflict of infancy with King Oedipus does not seem here to correspond to any clearly formulated theoretical considerations, but rather to have issued spontaneously from Freud's mind and then to have imposed itself by striking parallel in the

situations. This of course should not be taken to mean that the choice of term was without significance; on the contrary, we may presume that it served to emphasize the share of literature in the theoretical edifice and helped to propagate Freud's ideas outside Vienna. (In Switzerland, for example, the first country in which psychoanalysis gained non-Jewish disciples, this indication of a sound classical education may have opened a good many doors.) The term "complex" on the other hand, is not Freud's; it originated with the German psychiatrist Ziehen, in whom psychoanalysis was soon to find one of its worst enemies, and it was Jung who first used it in a strictly empirical sense (to designate the sensory and affective reactions indicating agitation in his association experiment). Psychoanalytic writers hesitated for a time between "Oedipus complex" and "father complex"; in Freud's letters to his first disciples "*Vatercomplex*" is more frequent.

[8] In view of the strongly Jewish character of Freud's work, some critics have expressed surprise, regret, or both that he should have invoked Greek rather than Jewish mythology in support of his theory. The Bible, says Éliane Amado Lévy-Valensi (*Les Voies et les pièges de la psychanalyse*, Paris, 1971) in substance, would have given him a more optimistic view of man than the myth of Oedipus. This accusation of pessimism comes as a surprise. When a man looks into the most hideous depths of human nature and not only preserves his faith as a physician but also believes to the very end in the final triumph of "our god Logos," might he not more plausibly be regarded as an incorrigible optimist? Moreover, the myth of Abraham and Isaac was not relevant to the situation Freud wished to illustrate. In the neurotic disorders of his patients he found no basis for such a parallel. He might have invoked it if his method had been different, if he had taken an idea rather than observation as his starting point. What he observed with the help of his special method was not a contest over a child between a human father and a divine father; what he observed was a flesh and blood parents arousing intense desires in a child.

NOTES

The myth of Oedipus, which Freud as a consummate humanist had at his disposal, was excellently suited to illustrating this situation.

⁴ Ludwig Binswanger, *Erinnerungen an Sigmund Freud*, Bern 1956, p. 13.

⁵ Freud, "On the History of the Psychoanalytic Movement," SE XIV, p. 47, n. 1. Adler is quoted as having said to Freud: "Do you think it is pleasant for me to vegetate all my life in your shadow?"

⁶ Of course the dividing line between the ideologies is not as sharp as I have made it appear. With the present simplification I have tried to bring out not so much the shadings of opinion as they developed over the years as the basic division at the beginning of the movement. The line of demarcation between Jews and non-Jews is expressly noted by Freud in a letter to Binswanger, the immediate occasion for which was Jung's attitude: "Only one thing is serious in all this: the Semites and the Aryans or anti-Semites, whom I hoped to unite in the service of psychoanalysis, are separating like oil and water . . ." (Op. cit., p. 60). On the other hand, Jones, a non-Jew, gave evidence of robust intellectual health in all these questions, while Ferenczi had a strong tendency to mystical speculation. Freud himself had always believed in premonitions, significant numbers, mysterious coincidences, and the transmission of thought, in short, in all the phenomena which the Surrealists were later to designate as "objective chance." The truth of the matter is that he often oscillated between *affective* credulity in response to intense experience and *intellectual* credulity toward the occult interpretation of facts. His polemic with Jung, who had come out in favor of ghosts and poltergeists, is characteristic in this respect (C. G. Jung, *Memories, Dreams, Reflections*, New York, 1963, pp. 361ff.). Under the influence of Ferenczi, whom he was very fond of, he developed a keen interest in the problems of spiritism and occultism, which were all the rage at the time. On several occasions Jones warned Freud against these excursions into parapsychology, rightly fearing

that they could cast discredit on the movement (Jones, III, pp. 375ff., especially p. 381). To the end of his life Freud was at once fascinated and repelled by the little mysteries of everyday life, but despite his marked tendency to credulity he was always careful not to raise the irrational to the level of reason. The passion with which he observed occult phenomena was no doubt revealing, but he never let it affect his theoretical conclusions. The best proof of this is provided precisely by his excursions into telepathy, for what he finally published on the subject ("Dreams and Telepathy," SE XVIII, pp. 197ff.) contains no statement that might not have found a place in his more classical work.

[7] L. Binswanger, op. cit., p. 98. These words from a conversation that took place in September 1927 are underlined by Binswanger.

[8] *Letters*, letter of October 8, 1936, to Ludwig Binswanger, p. 431.

[9] L. Binswanger, op. cit., p. 48. The phrase is underlined by the author.

[10] Jones II, pp. 353ff.

[11] Jones (II, p. 354) records Freud's pretexts for postponing publication of his *Totem and Taboo*. When Jones expressed his surprise that the author of the *Traumdeutung* could be so cautious, Freud replied: "Then I described the wish to kill one's father, and now I have been describing the actual killing: after all it is a big step from a wish to a deed."

[12] First published anonymously in the journal *Imago*, "The *Moses* of Michelangelo" did not appear under Freud's name until ten years later in the ten-volume edition of the *Gesammelte Werke*.

[13] "The *Moses* of Michelangelo," SE XIII, p. 213.
[14] "The *Moses* of Michelangelo," SE XIII, pp. 220f.

[15] Actually the main body of the essay has more to do with the problem of guilt than is generally supposed. The central question is whether or not Moses is represented at the mo-

ment when, infuriated by his people's worship of the Golden Calf, he is about to rise up and let the Tables of the Law slip from his grasp. Freud shows brilliantly that the gestures—the fingers in the beard, the arm holding back the Tables—do not allow of such an interpretation. Moses is not about to leap from his seat, for the most violent moment of his anger has passed. He almost let himself be carried away, but he was able to check his passion. Michelangelo portrays him after he has recovered his calm—a fact in which Freud finds cause for reassurance.

[16] Letter of May 28, 1933. *Letters*, p. 419.

[17] Letter of September 30, 1934. *Letters*, p. 421.

[18] Cf. above, p. 35, Freud's condolence letter of April 19, 1936, to Barbara Low after the death of avid Eder. At that time Freud had broken off his *Moses*, but he never stopped thinking about it and, as we see here, he continued to believe that the "mysterious thing" (which makes the Jew) was "inaccessible to any analysis."

[19] *Letters*, pp. 421f.

[20] Freud first published the two first chapters in the journal *Imago*, "Moses an Egyptian" in *Imago*, Vol. 23, No. I, Vienna 1937, and "If Moses was an Egyptian" in *Imago*, Vol. 23, No. IV, Vienna 1937.

[21] *Letters*, p. 422.

[22] Letter of November 6, 1934. *Freud/A. Zweig Letters*, p. 97.

[23] Letter of December 16, 1934. *Freud/A. Zweig Letters*, p. 98. [Translation slightly modified.]

[24] The humanity and masculinity of Moses are stressed both in the original title: "Der Mann Moses, ein historischer Roman" ("The Man Moses, a Historical Novel") and in the definitive title that replaced it: *Der Mann Moses and die monotheistische Religion* (*The Man Moses and Monotheism*).

[25] Letter of May 2, 1935. *Freud/A. Zweig Letters*, p. 106.

[26] Letter of June 13, 1935. *Freud/A. Zweig Letters*, p. 107.

[27] Letter to N.N. of December 14, 1937. *Letters*, p. 439.

[28] Letter of April 28, 1938. Jones III, p. 225.

[29] Freud, "Negation," SE XIX, pp. 235ff.

[30] Between 1934 and 1938 it was possible to regard the persecutions as more or less comparable to those of the past, and by and large this was the view held outside of Germany. The Nuremberg laws were promulgated in 1935, but though Jews already felt their effects, they were still free to travel, to frequent certain public places, and to emigrate. In 1936 the Olympic Games brought a respite; the persecutions did not resume until after the last foreign tourist had left the country. But the real terror began only with the *Kristallnacht* in November 1938, when numerous synagogues and Jewish shops were attacked and thousands of Jews were arrested.

[31] Freud, "Moses and Monotheism," SE XXIII, p. 7.

[32] "Moses and Monotheism," SE XXIII, p. 16.

[33] In a letter to Freud of November 22, 1935, Arnold Zweig deplores the ineptitude of German critics, and writes: "If only a man like you would devote a few months to reviewing novels." In this connection he mentions the two first novels of his friend Lion Feuchtwanger's trilogy: *Der jüdische Krieg* (1932), *Die Söhne* (1935), *Der Tag will kommen* (1945), the plot of which revolves around Josephus, the historian of the Jewish war against Titus (A.D. 70). He also speaks of Heinrich Mann's novel about Henri IV King of France *Die Jugend des Königs Henri Quatre* (Amsterdam, 1935). Sigmund Freud/Arnold Zweig, *Briefwechsel*, ed. Ernst L. Freud (Frankfurt, 1968), p. 122.

[34] *Freud/A. Zweig Letters*, pp. 79ff. Zweig had asked Freud to ask Lou Andreas-Salomé to supply him with details of her intimate life with Nietzsche. Freud had first refused, then complied, knowing in advance that his request would be futile.

[85] Letter of November 29, 1936. *Letters,* pp. 432f.

[36] On the Shakespeare question see Jones III, pp. 432f.

[37] This letter to Martha, quoted by Jones (III, p. 428) is not included in *Letters.*

[38] Jones, III, 428f.

[39] Jones, III, p. 429.

[40] Jones, III, p. 429.

[41] "Address Delivered in the Goethe House at Frankfurt," SE XXI, pp. 208ff.

[42] "An Autobiographical Study," SE XX, pp. 63f., n. 1.

[43] Cf. Freud's letter of June 22, 1938, to his brother Alexander, in which he describes his first contact with true fame. *Letters,* pp. 447f.

[44] Jones III, p. 198. This passage does not appear in the published letter (dated June 13, 1935, in *Freud/A. Zweig Letters,* pp. 107ff.) nor is there any indication that anything has been omitted. Here we can only rely on Jones, who had the whole letter at his disposal.

[45] *Freud/A. Zweig Letters,* p. 122. [Translation slightly modified.]

[46] Letter of January 17, 1938, to Ernst Freud. *Letters,* p. 440.

[47] Adolphe Lods, *Histoire de la littérature hébraïque et juive* (Paris, 1930), p. 12.

[48] *Moses and Monotheism,* SE XXIII, p. 27, n. 2. Author's italics.

[49] Adolphe Lods, *Israël des origines au milieu du VIII siècle* (Paris, 1930), p. 358; 1969 edition, p. 308.

[50] Freud seems to have found the theory that Moses was murdered by the Jews in a book by Ernst Sellin, *Mose und seine Bedeutung für die israelitisch-judische Religionsgeschichte* (1922). The author based his theory on a reinterpretation of certain passages in Hosea. Violently attacked by Jewish scholars, he is said to have retracted (according to one version seven and to another ten years later)

and to have apologized for having put forward a hypothesis so ill founded. When Professor Shalom Jahuda called on Freud in London in 1938, and pleaded with him not to publish his *Moses*, he told him of Sellin's retraction. According to Jones, III, p. 373, Freud only shrugged his shoulders and said: "It might be true all the same." Actually he had no need of Sellin as a reference; he could have found older, if not more scientific authority for the murder theory in Jewish folklore. Jones, for example, cites: Meyer Abraham, *La Mort de Moïse, Légendes juives apocryphes sur la vie de Moïse* (1925); Louis Ginzberg, *The Legends of the Jews* (1947); M. Rosenfeld, *Der Midrasch über den Tod des Moses* (1899).

[51] The *Moses* is a kind of compendium of the basic Freudian theories—Oedipus complex, castration complex, repression as pathogenic factor and force for civilization, sublimation, the "family novel," the "return of the repressed," the hereditary transmission of acquired characteristics, etc.—concerning the relations of the human individual with the man-made laws of civilizations.

[52] *Moses and Monotheism*, SE XXIII, p. 125. [Translation slightly modified.]

LIST OF WORKS
FREQUENTLY CITED

Freud, Sigmund

"Address Delivered in the Goethe House at Frankfurt" (1930), SE XXI.

"Address to the Society of B'nai B'rith" (1926), SE XX.

An Autobiographical Study (1924), with "Postscript" (1935), SE XX.

"Charcot" (1893), SE III.

Civilization and Its Discontents (1920), SE XXI.

"A Disturbance of Memory on the Acropolis" (1936), SE XXII.

Freud/Abraham Letters=A Psycho-Analytic Dialogue: The Letters of Sigmund Freud and Karl Abraham 1907–1926. Edited by Hilda C. Abraham and Ernst L. Freud; translated by Bernard Marsh and Hilda C. Abraham. London and New York, 1965.

Freud/Pfister Letters=Psycho-Analysis and Faith: The Letters of Sigmund Freud and Oskar Pfister. Edited by Heinrich Meng and Ernst L. Freud; translated by Eric Mosbacher. London and New York, 1963.

Freud/A. Zweig Letters=The Letters of Sigmund Freud and Arnold Zweig. Edited by Ernst L. Freud; translated by Professor and Mrs. W. D. Robson-Scott. London and New York, 1970.

"Group Psychology and the Analysis of the Ego" (1921), SE XVIII.

The Interpretation of Dreams (1900), SE IV-V.

"Josef Popper-Lynkeus and the Theory of Dreams" (1923), SE XIX.

Letters=Letters of Sigmund Freud. Selected and edited Ernst L. Freud; translated by Tania and James Stern. London and New York, 1960.

Moses and Monotheism (1934–38), SE XXIII.

"The Moses of Michelangelo" (1914), SE XIII.

"Negation" (1925), SE XIX.

"On Dreams" (1901), SE V.

Origins=The Origins of Psycho-Analysis: Letters to Wilhelm Fliess, Drafts and Notes, 1897–1902. Edited by Marie Bonaparte, Anna Freud, and Ernst Kris; authorized translation by Eric Mosbacher and James Strachey. New York and London, 1954.

An Outline of Psychoanalysis (1938), SE XXIII.

The Psychopathology of Everyday Life (1901), SE VI.

SE=*The Standard Edition of the Complete Psychological Works of Sigmund Freud*. Translated under the general editorship of James Strachey, in collaboration with Anna Freud, assisted by Alix Strachey and Alan Tyson. 24 vols., London and New York, 1953–74.

"Some Reflections on Schoolboy Psychology" (1914), SE XIII.

Jones I, II, III=Ernest Jones, *Sigmund Freud: Life and Work*, 3 vols., New York and London, 1953, 1955, 1957.

INDEX